Richborough ar

Tony Wilmott

CONTENTS

Tour of Richborough

SITE OVERVIEW

Though now 3km inland, in Roman times Richborough was a coastal site on the Wantsum Channel (see page 7). The Roman army dug ditches and made a rampart here to defend their invasion beachhead in AD 43. The site subsequently became a military supply base, then, after AD 70, an extensive port town known as Rutupiae. Remains of stone-built shops and the sites of timber buildings from this period can be seen. Richborough, as the official gateway to Roman Britain, was marked by one of the largest monumental arches in the Roman Empire, built about AD 85. The gravelled rectangle and raised 'cross' in the centre of the site mark its foundations. Three ditches were cut through the town buildings in the mid third century to fortify the monument. These were filled in and replaced in the later third century by the massive walls of a Saxon Shore fort. This was occupied for a further 150 years before the site was abandoned by the Roman army.

The tour first explores the later third-century fort walls and then the interior, examining the various features inside it in roughly chronological order.

Above: Roman weapons found at Richborough include a tanged socketed iron spearhead (left) and a large tanged arrowhead (right)

Below: *Aerial view of Richborough looking south-east towards the site of the amphitheatre (in the circular field). The Roman shoreline probably followed the approximate line of the eastern bank of the river*

Facing page: *Detail of the wall of the Saxon Shore fort. The original facing stones and the 'putlog' holes, which held timber scaffolding posts during construction, can be seen towards the top*

South wall of the Saxon Shore fort

A *Wall core of flint, stones and concrete*

B *Original facing stones*

C *Foundation of the rectangular interval tower*

D *Hole made by post-Roman stone robbers*

E *South-west corner tower*

F *Inner ditch of the Saxon Shore fort*

Below: On the north wall of the fort the point where the brown ironstone chequer work abruptly ends marks the point at which two building gangs, each working in a slightly different style, met

◾ SAXON SHORE FORT AND DITCHES

The most prominent features at Richborough are the defences of a late third-century Saxon Shore fort. This was one of a series of coastal installations protecting the Roman province of Britain from seaborne Saxon and Frankish raiders. The masonry wall, 3.3m thick at the base, survives in places to a height of 8m. This is probably close to the original height of a sentry-walk. A crenellated parapet would have provided protection for troops on the walls, and brought the full height up to some 10m. The walls of the fort originally formed a complete circuit. At some point before the 15th century, the cliff edge eroded and the eastern side of the fort collapsed. Large sections of wall now lie at the base of the embankment between the hillside and the railway line. Outside the walls was a pair of substantial ditches. The inner ditch was 10m wide and 3m deep, the outer, 8m wide and 2m deep. The fort walls encompass an area of 2.5ha and all the military buildings would have been enclosed within.

The wall originally had a core of coursed flint, stones and concrete, faced with stone blocks. The facing stone is best seen in the north-east corner of the fort where squared blocks of locally quarried limestone, sandstone and brown ironstone are interrupted by six 'bonding courses' of tile, which kept the stone and concrete level during construction. At some points the brown ironstone and limestone have been alternated to create a decorative chequered effect. Between bonding courses are rows of small 'putlog' holes, in which horizontal scaffold poles were placed during construction. Around the fort, most of the facing stone has been removed (archaeologists call this 'stone robbing') for use elsewhere, probably in the walls of the medieval buildings of nearby Sandwich. Stone robbers cut the large holes in the wall and undermined some sections to weaken it and speed its collapse.

Gates

In the centre of each side of the fort was a gate. The gap in the wall opposite the modern shop is the site of a south gate, which was probably a small postern. The west gate was the main landward entrance to the fort. It lies in the centre of the west wall, opposite the modern wooden bridge over the ditches. It was a single portal gate flanked by two projecting towers, and would have had rooms in the storey above the gate arch. The large foundation stones of the south tower are visible. A third ditch between the two main ditches at this point was probably the result of a Roman planning error, as it was filled in soon after it was dug. Roman Watling Street, the main road from Richborough to the provincial capital at London, passed through this gateway and across the ditches on a causeway.

The north postern gate, contained in the tower in the centre of the north wall, survives to almost full height. A concealed entrance in the east side of the tower gave access into the fort through a defensible dog-leg approach. No trace of the location of the original wooden door has survived.

Towers

Midway between each gate and the corners of the fort were rectangular projecting interval towers, and the corners themselves were furnished with circular projecting towers. The foundations of the interval towers can be seen, as well as 'scars' in the masonry where they joined the main fort wall. The corner towers may have been solid, with no internal rooms, and would have been used to mount arrow-firing artillery and to allow archers to fire across the face of the fort wall to prevent enemies scaling it. The interval towers were hollow, and the four large holes visible in the masonry of some of the towers at a high level would have held joists for an upper wooden floor within the tower. The ground-floor rooms, which were probably guard rooms, accommodation or stores, would have been reached by wooden stairs or ladders from above. The upper storeys were entered through doors from the sentry-walk. The sentry-walk itself was reached via

Features of the Saxon Shore fort

A *A fragment of Italian marble from the decorative cladding of the monumental arch. It was recycled near the interval tower in the north-west corner of the fort when the arch was broken up and the marble burned to make lime for the concrete used in the fort wall*

B *Remains of a sculpture of a lion in the outer wall of the north gate, recycled from an earlier building. The head is missing, but the hind-quarters and part of the mane are visible. It is known as 'Queen Bertha's Head' (see page 43)*

C *Looking north-east through the dog-leg of the north postern gate*

A

B

C

stairs in the towers of the principal gates. In the foundation of the interval tower to the north of the west gate, a gully lined with tiles in one corner was an outlet for a latrine. The original level, pebbled floor surface of the bottom storey can be seen upon the foundation of the interval tower between the north-east corner tower and the north postern gate.

2 CLAUDIAN INVASION DITCHES

In the north-west corner of the Saxon Shore fort are sections of two parallel ditches on each side of a gap. These are the earliest Roman features on the site, and were dug at the time of the Claudian invasion of Britain, in AD 43. They were laid out parallel to the coast, which ran close to the line taken by the river today. They were probably dug to defend troops, supplies and the ships of the fleet from potential attack while the initial invasion beachhead was established. Aerial photography and geophysical survey have traced the ditches running well beyond the walls of the later fort to both north and south, for a distance of at least 650m (see map page 31). The inner ditch was 3.5m wide and 2m deep, the outer somewhat smaller, and the ditches were 2m apart. There would have been a turf and earth rampart on the eastern side, with a timber parapet on top. The gap is the site of an entrance causeway, 3.25m wide, originally flanked by timber posts, which supported a timber tower. Looking back through the gate of the stone fort, which was built more than two centuries later, it is easy to see that the line of Watling Street must have been set at this very earliest period, when it was one of the routes created by the Roman army during the first years of the conquest.

Above: Reconstruction of the timber and earth defences of the invasion camp. The gateway marked the beginning of Watling Street
Right: A short section of the ditches dug to defend the invasion beachhead of AD 43

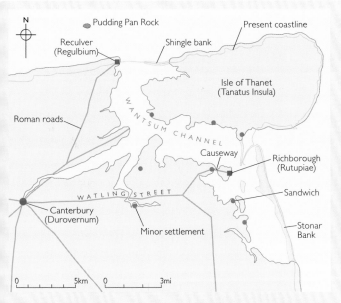

N

Pudding Pan Rock

Reculver
(Regulbium)

Shingle bank

Present coastline

Isle of Thanet
(Tanatus Insula)

Roman roads

WANTSUM CHANNEL

Causeway

Richborough
(Rutupiae)

WATLING STREET

Sandwich

Canterbury
(Durovernum)

Minor settlement

Stonar
Bank

0   5km   0   3mi

Left: Map of the Roman coastline of the Wantsum Channel with roads and settlements. The present coastline is marked with a pale blue line

The Wantsum Channel

The Wantsum Channel was formed about 8,000 years ago when sea levels rose at the end of the last glaciation. The channel separated the Isle of Thanet from the British mainland. The Stour and other rivers drained into this tidal channel. At the southern end the Stonar Bank, a shingle barrier created by longshore drift from the south, partially closed the mouth of the channel. Roman finds have been recovered from the bank, showing that its formation had begun by the Roman period. Richborough was therefore at the centre of a large anchorage, sheltered by the mainland, Thanet and the Stonar Bank. Another shingle bank formed across the mouth at the northern end. Reculver occupied a promontory site on the mainland at the northern end of the Wantsum, commanding a view of the mouth of the channel.

While the channel was open, the tide would have removed silt, but the shingle banks prevented this, and silt gradually accumulated. This would have started by the Roman period, although the channel remained navigable.

Sandwich probably replaced Richborough as the principal port from the seventh century. During the 14th century people were creating barriers in the Wantsum to collect silt and reclaim land. In 1484 a Spanish ship, presumably a hulk, was obstructing the passage, and in 1537 watercourses were blocked between Richborough and Sandwich impeding the waterflow into Sandwich Haven. A small waterfront at Richborough dating to the

15th century was probably used by small craft on the channel of the river Stour, and probably went out of use as the path taken by that river slowly shifted eastwards to its present course.

By the later 16th century the Wantsum Channel was completely silted. Today the flat, marshy land of the silted channel drains into the river Stour (to the east) and the river Wantsum (to the north), the latter being little more than a drainage ditch.

Above: Detail from a relief of the second to third century showing a sailing ship entering a harbour
Below: Samian ware imported from Gaul. This pottery was found on a Roman shipwreck on Pudding Pan Rock in the Thames Estuary north of Reculver

Right: The recreated horreum, or granary, at Lunt Roman Fort near Coventry. The granaries at Richborough would have been similar in size and construction, built in timber and raised on piles to discourage vermin

Below right: The site of a Roman shop. Situated on a street corner, the positions of its walls and the columns of its verandah have been marked in concrete

3 GRANARIES

After the Claudian invasion, in the period between AD 43 and AD 85, the beachhead ditches were filled in and a street grid was laid out. Twelve large, parallel, rectangular buildings measuring 28m by 9m were found, in three groups of four (see map page 33). Two of the buildings are marked out by concrete strips in the ground. These were granaries or stores housing supplies for the army as it advanced across Britain. When the army was able to supply itself from the resources of the province, these buildings may have become port warehouses.

4 FIRST-CENTURY SHOP

From about AD 70 Richborough became a civilian port to which Continental goods were imported and from which produce from Britain was exported. Some of the store buildings were demolished and replaced with timber shops (see map page 34). The position of one excavated shop, between the Claudian ditches and the west wall of the stone fort, is marked on site using concrete strips. This was a long, narrow, single-storey building with a shop in the front and living quarters to the rear. The shop was open to the street, where a roofed verandah supported on wooden columns provided shelter. Concrete circles now mark the positions of these columns.

First-century shop

Foundation trenches

Post holes

Posts

Living quarters

Verandah over side-street pavement

Shop

Verandah over street pavement

Posts

AD c.43–c.70

0 — 10m

0 — 30ft

N

Roman Board Games

Gambling was very popular in Roman times and dice and game boards are frequently found on sites throughout the Roman Empire. A number of finely decorated bone plaques found at Richborough have been interpreted as part of a *pyrgus* or dice tower. This comprised a box with a series of angled slats set inside. A die dropped in the top would bounce randomly on the slats and fall out of the bottom, making it impossible to cheat. It may have been used in games of *duodecim scripta* or *tabula* – games from which modern backgammon descends. The example found at Richborough is one of only three such objects to survive from the entire Roman Empire.

Game boards, often scratched on stones, flagstones or steps, and counters of pottery or stone are found more frequently. A chequered board from Richborough was carved onto a piece of the Italian marble taken from the demolished monumental arch.

The poet Juvenal, writing in the first to second century, satirized the Roman obsession with gaming: 'When was gambling so reckless? Men come not now with purses to the hazard of the gaming table, but with a treasure-chest beside them', *Satires* 1, 87–93.

Above left: *A third-century mosaic from Tunisia showing a board game in progress, with counters, dice and possibly a dice tower*

Above: *A reconstruction in wood of the decorated bone dice tower (pyrgus) from Richborough*

Below: *A game board made from Italian marble and pottery counters found at Richborough*

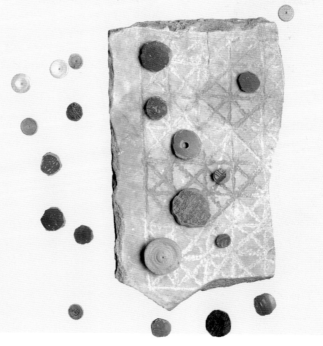

Below: Only a few hints survive of the decoration of the arch. These indicate that there were battle and naval scenes:

A A fragment of carved inscription
B The swan's head prow of a ship
C A fragment of bronze drapery

A

B

C

5 MONUMENTAL ARCH

In the centre of the fort is the site of one of the largest monumental arches in the Roman Empire, dating to about AD 85. Before the site was excavated, the large, raised, cross-shaped platform was the most prominent feature within the walls, and many people dug around it in order to try to understand it. Beneath the cross they found a massive foundation of layered flints and clay 10m deep. The gravelled rectangle shows the extent of this foundation.

Only in the mid 20th century was it realized that a four-way triumphal arch of the kind known as a '*quadrifrons*' once stood here. In its four corners stood enormous stone-built piers linked by arches, which spanned the arms of the cross. The arches on the east and west side (the short arms of the cross) were broader. Above the arches was a solid attic storey. The monument would have been 25m high. The cross formed the raised internal passageways through the arch, and there would have been a flight of steps at the end of each arm.

A large amount of white Italian marble from the imperial quarries at Carrara has been found, including fluted columns and other architectural elements, showing that the whole arch was faced in ornate marble cladding. The monument would also have been covered in sculpture and inscriptions in marble and bronze, scraps of which have survived. It may have

appeared even higher if a large equestrian statue or a *quadriga*, a four-horse chariot, had been placed on its flat top.

The arch marked the transition from sea to land and the beginning or end of a sea voyage. It might have been dedicated to Neptune or the god Ocean, and it is possible that its decoration reflected this. Richborough was the main entry point into Britain from the Continent, so the arch was also the symbolic gateway to Britain, aligned with the course of Watling Street. The arch at Ancona in Italy, built in AD 115 under the Emperor Trajan (r.AD 98–117), was similarly considered by the Romans as the gateway to Italy. The date of the Richborough arch, about AD 85, coincides with the completion of the conquest of Britain in the reign of the Emperor Domitian (r.AD 81–96), which the arch may also have celebrated (see page 35).

The monument stood for two centuries, until about AD 250, when it probably became a lookout to give early warning of seaborne raiders in the Wantsum Channel, as the threat of Saxon pirates from across the North Sea became greater. Later in the century (AD 275 to 300) the monument was demolished together with civilian buildings to make room for the Saxon Shore fort and its internal structures. The arch was also used as a supply of building material – the marble cladding was broken up and burned in kilns to produce lime needed for the concrete of the fort walls (see page 5).

Above: Reconstruction of the great monumental arch as seen from the waterfront at Richborough in about AD 120. In its elevated position by the sea, the monument would probably have been visible from as far as halfway across the English Channel. It would have acted as a marker for cross-Channel shipping as well as forming a ceremonial entrance to the Roman province of Britannia

Top: The original wall lines of the south-west corner of later mansio *buildings have been marked in the grass with concrete strips*
Above: *Decorated tablewares, such as this Samian vessel imported to Richborough from Gaul, were likely to have been used in the* mansio

6 OFFICIAL INN (*MANSIO*)

A series of courtyard buildings of several phases is located in the north-east corner of the fort. The first structure was a large wooden courtyard house, probably for the military official in charge of the first-century supply base. This was replaced in stone in about AD 70. No remains of either building are visible.

After the arch was erected in about AD 85, the courtyard house was rebuilt further to the north-east. The remains of this building can be seen on site. It included a small bath-house, and was probably a *mansio*, or inn for official travellers. *Mansiones* were built along the main roads to provide accommodation and stabling for those using the imperial courier service (*cursus publicus*). *Mansio* complexes usually comprised suites of rooms set round a courtyard with a bath-house either integral to the main building or very near to it. A *mansio* would have been essential at a major port such as Richborough. It was rebuilt again in the early second century and retained into the third century, avoiding destruction by the building of a defensive ditch that cut through other structures. By that point it may again have been the residence of a military commander.

The walls of the building project beyond the line of the stone fort walls, and much of it was demolished when the Saxon Shore fort was built in the late third century.

Official inn (*mansio*)

AD c.50
AD c.70
AD c.90
AD c.125

Paler shades indicate possible courtyard layouts

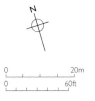

0   20m
0   60ft

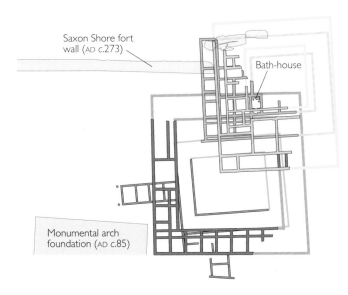

Saxon Shore fort wall (AD c.273)

Bath-house

Monumental arch foundation (AD c.85)

Travelling in the Empire

The ability to travel throughout the Empire was fundamental to how it functioned. Tombstones show that people lived and died in provinces far from their origins, and this did not only apply to the soldiers on the imperial frontiers. Traders introduced a bewildering variety of products throughout the Empire. Bulky goods were usually transported by sea or river rather than by road in ox-drawn wagons.

In administering the Empire, the capacity to carry messages swiftly through the imperial courier service, known as the *cursus publicus*, was important. Road stations known as *mansiones* or *stationes* were set up at regular intervals to provide accommodation and fresh mounts for the couriers. These establishments, often including a much needed bath-house, also provided lodgings for other travellers.

Guides to the *cursus publicus* existed in the form of road books or itineraries. Of these, the Peutinger Table is the only copy of a Roman map to survive. The Antonine Itinerary lists routes between named places. The only Channel crossing listed in this official document is that from Boulogne to Richborough.

The poet Horace, writing in the first century BC, gives a humorous account of the various hazards of undertaking a journey south of Rome in *Satire 1, V*. He gets a stomach bug from drinking brackish water, is kept awake by frogs, mosquitoes and drunks, rain damages the roads and a girl he has high hopes for fails to show up. At one place he was staying, he and his companions almost ended up as burned as the food when the kitchen caught fire.

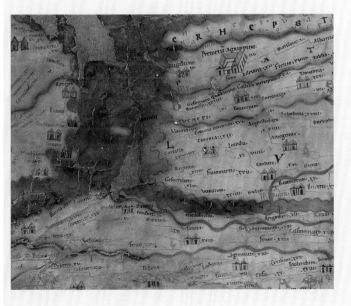

Above: A sculptured panel from a sarcophagus showing members of the imperial courier service (cursus publicus) arriving at a mansio
Left: Extract from the Peutinger Table, a medieval copy of an original Roman map of about the fourth or early fifth century, showing the ports of the English Channel, including 'Ratupis' (Richborough)

Below: One of the second-century shops sold ceramic oil lamps like this one found at Richborough

Bottom: The centre of the Saxon Shore fort with the foundation of the arch to the left, and the southern fort wall in the distance. The foundations of the second-century building in the centre have been cut through by the mid third-century defensive ditches

▇ SECOND-CENTURY TOWN BUILDINGS

The large port town at Richborough was probably at its greatest extent in the late first to later second century. Several features of the town from this period are visible (see map page 34).

In the north-west corner of the site are the foundations of stone buildings – shops built on the Watling Street frontage. Like their timber predecessors, they were open at the front with rooms behind for storage and accommodation. One of these appears to have sold lamps, and there is evidence for metalworking in this area. Much of the town, and certainly most of the street frontages in the centre, would have been used for this kind of shop or workshop, some of which would have been built in stone and some in timber depending on the prosperity of the owner. The remains of another stone building can be seen on the high points between the three ditches surrounding the monument, showing that the ditches were cut straight through the building. It is probable that the shops and houses were still in use when these ditches were dug, and that they were cleared because of military necessity.

▇ MID THIRD-CENTURY DITCHES

The imposing triple ditches that cut so dramatically through the walls of the stone shop building were dug in the mid third century to surround the monument, although they stopped short of the *mansio* building (see map page 38). These additions turned the monument into a military installation. There would have been an earth rampart inside these ditches, probably with a timber parapet. The only known gate is where

the ditches are interrupted on the line of Watling Street. By the time these were dug, the town appears to have been shrinking. Perhaps it was suffering from commercial competition from the ports of London and Dover. The fortification of the monument, however, removed a large section of the centre of the town, and it is possible to visualize the army hastily requisitioning buildings for demolition.

The ditched fortification probably lasted only 25–30 years before the ditches were filled in, the monumental arch demolished, and the stone fort built after about AD 273, using still more of the land that had once been the centre of the town.

Above: A bone comb and tweezers found at Richborough, typical toilet instruments used in a bath-house
Below: The third-century bath-house. The stoke-hole for the hypocaust can be seen in the foreground

9 BATH-HOUSE

The highest standing remains in the north-east corner of the site are those of a small bath-house built for the Saxon Shore fort. This is one of the very few internal fort buildings that have been recognized – possibly because it was one of the only stone buildings within the walls. It would have served the whole fort garrison. It is a very simple building, reusing the remains of the earlier walls of the *mansio* in its construction. It consisted of three principal rooms: first a combined vestibule and changing room (*apodyterium*), from which opened a small cold plunge-bath and a warm room (*tepidarium*), beyond which was a hot room (*caldarium*). The latter two rooms were heated by an underfloor hypocaust, the fire for which was placed in a stoke-hole by the wall of the *caldarium*. It is not known how long the building remained in use, but it was probably abandoned with the rest of the fort some time in the fifth century.

Bath-house

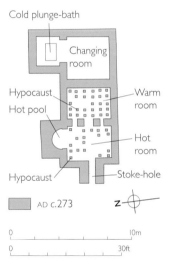

Cold plunge-bath
Changing room
Hypocaust
Hot pool
Warm room
Hot room
Hypocaust
Stoke-hole
AD c.273

0 — 10m
0 — 30ft

Top: The remains of a fourth-century hexagonal baptismal font

Above: A late Roman pottery vessel found at Richborough on which the Christian symbol of the 'chi-rho' has been scratched

Below: The poorly preserved medieval chapel of St Augustine. Where the walls do not survive, their lines are marked in the grass in concrete

10 ROMAN BAPTISMAL FONT

In the north-west corner of the fort is a small hexagonal structure made of tile. This was the baptismal font of a Roman Christian church. No other traces of this, the latest known Roman building on the site, can be seen, but it seems to have been a simple, rectangular timber structure constructed against the fort wall, possibly as a lean-to. The font may have been housed in a small side-chapel or baptistery, though no traces of an enclosing structure remain. This is one of the very rare Christian structures in Roman Britain to survive from the period when Christianity became first legal, and later the official religion of the Roman Empire, during the fourth century. This building too was abandoned with the rest of the fort.

11 CHAPEL OF ST AUGUSTINE

The building outlined on the raised area to the east of the monument, just within the mid third-century ditches, is a medieval chapel dedicated to St Augustine. The first church comprised a nave with a rectangular chancel to the east and a small western annexe – possibly a porch. This probably dates to the tenth century, but may have had a timber predecessor, possibly built as early as the seventh century. In the 12th century the chancel was enlarged and provided with an apse, and a further small annexe was added to the west end. The remains were so fragmentary that the later history of the building is not known, though documents show that it remained in use until the 17th century. Though the chapel appears to have stood in isolation in the centre of the abandoned Roman fort, it may have been linked to the continuing use of the site as a small port on the river. Excavations on the slope to the east of the chapel showed that during the 15th century the chapel stood above a small riverside dock with buildings using the fallen Saxon Shore fort wall as a foundation.

12 AMPHITHEATRE

Located on a slight rise to the south-west of the later Saxon
Shore fort, the amphitheatre at Richborough was first identified
in the 18th century and was partially excavated in 1848. Recent
geophysical surveys have revealed that it comprised an oval
arena 62m long by 50m wide. The arena was surrounded by a
stone wall and performers would have entered it at either end.
Surrounding the arena, 10m-wide raised banks supported seating
from where the audience would have looked down onto the
action. Although its exact date is not known, its typical position at
the edge of the urban area suggests that the Roman town at
Richborough had already reached its full extent before it was built.
Its size might suggest a maximum audience of 4,000–5,000 people.

As a newly established port town, Richborough's population
would have included people from across the Empire who would
have regarded the provision of amphitheatre spectacles as a
normal part of civilized life. Like all amphitheatres Richborough's
arena would have hosted wild beast hunts, probably featuring
mainly native species – bulls, wild boars and bears. The execution
of criminals and fights between gladiators would also have taken
place here. Amphitheatres were often surrounded by food stalls
and shops selling souvenirs for the spectators.

'In any exhibition of
gladiators ... if any of the
combatants chanced to fall,
he [Emperor Claudius]
ordered them to be
butchered, especially the
Retiarii, that he might see
their faces in the agonies
of death.' Suetonius, *Life
of Claudius*, 34

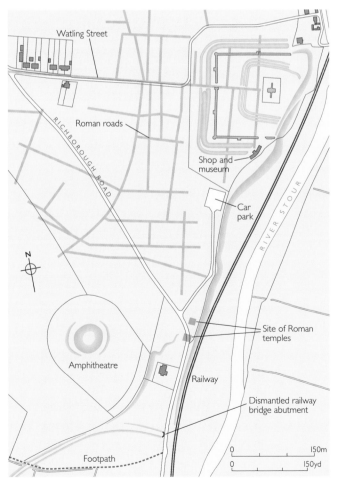

*Above: Fragment of a painted glass
bowl from Vindolanda on Hadrian's
Wall. It shows combat between
a heavily armed secutor gladiator,
armed with a sword, shield and
helmet, and a retiarius, armed
with a trident and a net. The
referee (summa rudis) can be seen
on the left, wearing a tunic and
waving a rod*
*Left: Map of Richborough showing
the locations of the roads of the
Roman town and the amphitheatre*

Tour of Reculver

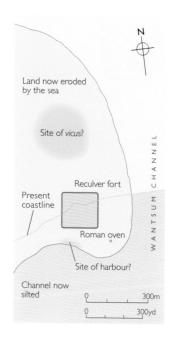

SETTING AND LAYOUT

The Roman fort at Reculver was built in the later second or early third century. Its purpose was to overlook and guard the north entry to the Wantsum Channel from the North Sea and Thames Estuary. This wide sea channel to the south and east of the site has now silted completely. To the north of the fort, about 1km away, was the sea coast. This eroded gradually and inexorably from Roman times until finally, in the late 18th century, much of the northern and western sides of the fort itself were lost to the sea. The cliff is now stabilized with sea defences.

Reculver fort appears to be one of the earliest garrisons in the coastal chain that later became known as the Saxon Shore. The fort was built to the conventional Roman plan, common to all forts built during the first and second centuries. It was basically square with rounded corners and gates halfway along all four sides. The gate towers stood within the wall of the fort, and the entire interior was filled with military buildings. The fort was surrounded by ditches. Only the southern and eastern outer walls of the fort have survived coastal erosion, and are visible. Within the fort, the church also has a long history, dating to Anglo-Saxon times. The original church of 669 was constantly expanded and developed until the 15th century, including the addition of the towers in the 12th century. The church was demolished in 1809.

Above: Map showing the position of Reculver in Roman times on a headland in the Wantsum Channel
Below: Aerial photograph of Reculver looking north, showing the surviving area of the fort enclosure

Facing page: The Reculver towers, known as the 'Two Sisters', loom over the modern sea defences

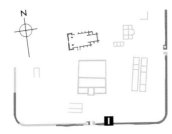

▮ WALLS OF THE ROMAN FORT

The path between the south side of the King Ethelbert Inn and the caravan park runs adjacent to the south wall of the third-century Roman fort. Its stonework can be seen in the hedge bank. As at Richborough, the facing stone was removed by stone robbers from about the fifth century onwards, and only the flint and concrete of the core remains. The wall, which once stood 4.5m high, would have had an earth rampart built against the inside face and was surmounted by a wall-walk and a parapet. Two ditches spaced 10m and 20m from the wall surrounded the fort, but no traces of these are visible today.

Halfway along the south wall is the site of the south gate. The remains of the gateway and one guard chamber are visible in the bank. One large stone has a hole in it, which housed a pivot on which the inward-opening wooden gate swung. This side of the fort overlooked the Roman harbour in the Wantsum Channel, which was located where the caravans are now.

The south-east corner of the fort is rounded with no external tower. The east gate was halfway along the eastern wall of the fort. It was a single portal 2.7m wide flanked by two internal towers. The guard chamber in the base of the northern gate tower can be seen. The modern path into the fort follows the main street (*via principalis*), which ran directly between the east and the west gates. Excavations here revealed that the east gate was blocked some time in the late third or fourth century. The Anglo-Saxon church was built with material reused from the Roman wall of the fort – for example, all of the red tile in the standing remains of the church is Roman in origin. The rest of the stone from the walls would probably have been reused in building the later village of Reculver, though no reused stones are visible today.

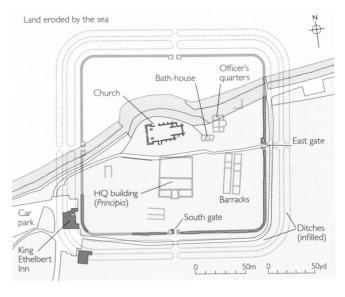

Above: The fragmentary remains of the south wall of the fort
Right: Plan of the fort of Reculver showing the locations of Roman buildings known from excavation

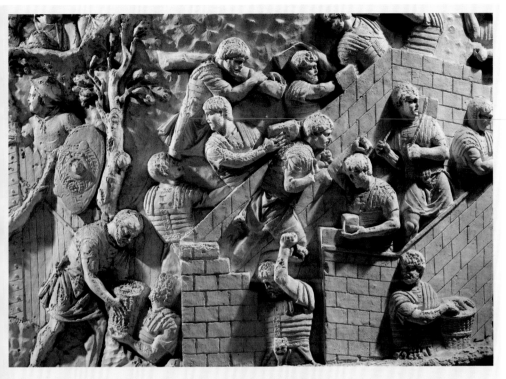

The Changing Design of Roman Forts

Reculver is typical of the Roman forts of the first and second centuries. These forts were rectangular with rounded corners – the so-called 'playing card' shape. The walls were narrow and backed by a substantial earth rampart. Such forts had at least four gates, most of which had two portals. They were flanked by small internal square towers and there were internal towers around the walls and at the corners. The interior of the fort was built up to a fairly standard plan, including a headquarters building, commander's residence, barracks, granaries, and stores, and perhaps a hospital. Bath-houses were usually outside the walls. These forts were not primarily designed to be defensive, as the strategy of the earlier

Roman army was to leave the fort and to bring an enemy to battle in the open field. Around most forts a civilian settlement or *vicus* grew up, where the dependants of the army unit lived, and where traders and other services were located.

The Saxon Shore fort at Richborough is typical of a later fort type. It was intended to be defensible against attackers with siege equipment. The massive concrete and

masonry walls were very much thicker and higher than those of early forts. The main gates were single rather than double portal, and were reduced in number, though small postern gates were provided. Bastions were built on the external faces of the walls to allow defenders to shoot at attackers attempting to scale them. The internal layout of the later forts is poorly understood, but was probably not regular and no evidence for extensive civilian settlements around these later forts has been found.

Top: Soldiers building a fort in a scene from the early second-century Trajan's Column, Rome
Above: Some building tools found at Richborough: a carpenter's adze (top) and a hand hammer (bottom)

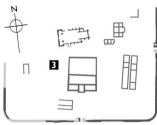

☑ OUTSIDE THE ROMAN FORT

The low land to the east of the fort was once the seaway of the Wantsum Channel, which has now completely silted. Roman Reculver directly overlooked the channel and a small harbour may have been tucked under its south wall. A large structure thought to be a drying oven for corn or other foodstuffs, such as fish, was also found in this area, about 60m from the south-east corner of the fort, outside the defensive ditches. To the north and west of the fort a civilian settlement (*vicus*) existed, most of which has been lost to erosion. The extent of this settlement is unknown, but as this was never a major port, it would have been much smaller than the town at Richborough, being intended only to service the needs of the garrison.

Below: Part of a Samian *mortarium with a spout in the form of a lion's head, used for grinding and mixing food.* Mortaria *were a new type of vessel introduced to Britain by the Romans*

☑ INTERIOR OF THE ROMAN FORT

Excavations during the 1960s showed that the whole of the interior of the fort was built to the standard early Roman fort plan (see page 21). On the south side of the path that now crosses the site there were at least two barrack blocks, each

The Garrison at Reculver

An important stone tablet was found in the headquarters building. The inscription records the construction of the shrine (*aedes*) where the regimental standards were kept, probably by the

auxiliary infantry unit known as the *cohors I Baetasiorum* (or the first cohort formed from the tribe of the Baetasii from northern Germany). This regiment had served in Scotland and garrisoned forts

on Hadrian's Wall. In the later second century it was at Maryport on the coast of Cumbria, and was then transferred to Reculver, where tiles stamped with the garrison's initials 'CIB' were found during excavations.

The inscription reads: 'Fortunatus [built] the shrine in the headquarters with the cross-hall under the consular governor [A Triarius] Rufinus'. It tells us that when the *aedes* was built, the fort commander was Fortunatus, and the provincial governor was Rufinus, whose exact dates in the early third century are unknown.

Left: A reconstruction of the inscription from surviving fragments. The letters are picked out in red, as they may have been in Roman times

housing 32 men; a further building, the purpose of which is unknown; and the headquarters building (*principia*). The *principia* comprised an open courtyard, behind which lay a cross-hall or *basilica* in which the official business of the regiment was conducted. Behind this was a range of offices flanking the shrine (*aedes*), where the official religion of the imperial cult was celebrated, and where the standards of the regiment were displayed. Beneath the *aedes* was an underfloor strong-room in which the pay chests for the regiment would have been securely stored.

A road (*via praetoria*) led from the front entrance of the *principia* to the north gate. This shows that the design of the fort faced north, towards the Thames Estuary, then a kilometre away. To the north of the modern path was a small bath-house for the use of the garrison. This was an unusual arrangement, as bath-houses were normally located outside the walls in early forts. Other buildings in the fort would have included more barracks, store buildings, the *praetorium*, or residence of the commanding officer, and possibly a *valetudinarium* or hospital.

Reconstruction of the Roman fort at Reculver looking east

A *Isle of Thanet*
B *Wantsum Channel*
C *Barracks*
D *Headquarters building (principia), consisting of an open courtyard, the* basilica *and the* aedes
E *The* via praetoria *leading to the north gate of the fort*
F *North gate*
G *Bath-house*
H *Civilian settlement (vicus)*

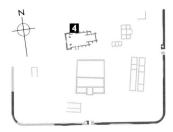

Right: A cutaway model to show the structure of the church at Reculver as built in 669. No evidence survives for the decoration of the interior, though it is likely that the walls were richly painted

Below: A 19th-century photograph of the chancel columns from Reculver church re-erected in Canterbury. Canterbury Cathedral can just be seen in the background behind the trees. The columns are now in the cathedral crypt

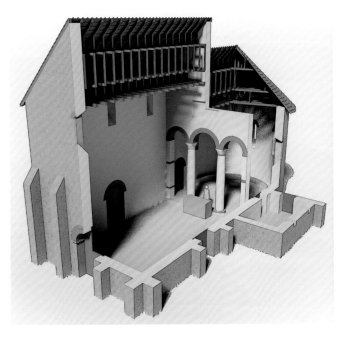

◪ SAXON AND LATER CHURCH

In 669, some two centuries after the Roman fort was abandoned, an Anglo-Saxon church was built within the walls of the old Roman fort. This was not an uncommon occurrence; churches were also built at the Saxon Shore forts of Bradwell-on-Sea on the Essex coast and also at Richborough (see page 16). The church was the centre of a monastic complex at Reculver, but the associated buildings of the monastery have long since disappeared, either because they were built of timber, or owing to stone robbing.

The large rectangular area marked out in concrete edged with flint is the nave of the first church, founded by Abbot Bassa in 669. The congregation gathered for services in the nave, which had entrances to west, north and south. To the east, the sites of two column bases are marked. The columns supported three semi-circular arches separating the nave from the apsidal chancel, which was reserved for the clergy. In front of the central arch, in the nave, stood the seventh-century

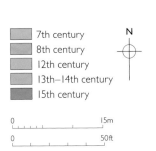

7th century
8th century
12th century
13th–14th century
15th century

N

0   15m
0   50ft

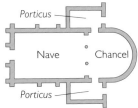

7th century

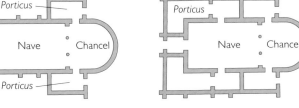

8th century

Reculver Cross (although some now think that it dates to the ninth century), an elaborately carved monument some 3m high. It was still standing in 1540. The original columns and fragments of the cross are preserved in the crypt of Canterbury Cathedral. The two side chapels (or *porticus*) flanking the chancel arch are original. In Anglo-Saxon churches *porticus* formed rudimentary transepts and were often used for burials, although there is no evidence for burials at Reculver. Parts of their walls stand 2m high, and clearly visible in the north *porticus* are the bases of two typical seventh-century windows with splayed internal sills and sides. The brick and tile visible in these early walls was reused from the Roman fort.

In the eighth century additional *porticus* were added. Missing walls are marked out on site by strips of concrete surfaced with broken flint. These consisted of one chapel to the west of each primary *porticus*, and L-shaped rooms round each western corner of the first church. The area between these extensions formed a western porch.

Above: Reculver church looking north-west. The 12th-century towers and the 13th-century chancel frame the remains of the original church
Below: One of the windows of the seventh-century north *porticus*, with a splayed internal sill

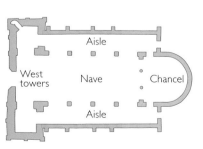

12th century

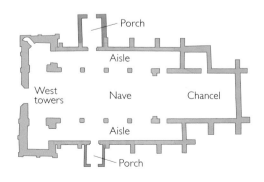

13th century and later

Above: Detail of the blocked west door of the 12th-century church

Below: A 19th-century engraving of a lost 17th-century map of Reculver showing the church with its tall spires standing in the middle of the fort enclosure before the northern half was lost to sea erosion

Facing page: View from the east showing the precarious coastal location of the Reculver towers, and highlighting their importance as a navigation mark

The church retained this shape for four centuries, until the towers were constructed at the end of the 12th century. On the tops of the towers wooden spires were built, as shown in 18th-century engravings. At the same time, the walls dividing the *porticus* were demolished, creating a pair of aisles, the single-pitch roof-lines of which can be seen above the ground-floor doors in the two towers. This would have allowed a larger congregation to assemble under one roof, and may reflect an increase in the village population. The nave of the church was entered through an ornamented west door between the two towers, which has since been blocked. The tower nearest the sea incorporates a stair from which all three floors could be reached.

The eastern end of the building was modified in the 13th century, when the apse of the original chancel was demolished and a new, extended, square chancel with an entrance porch on the north side was added. The chancel had a triple window facing east, decorated with Purbeck marble columns. Finally, in the 15th century, southern and northern porches were added to allow access into the western end of the nave.

The building continued for centuries as the parish church, complete with graveyard, from which some gravestones survive. By 1781, however, erosion had caused the north-west corner of the fort to fall into the sea and the church to become unsafe to use. Most of it was blown up with gunpowder in 1809, leaving only the western towers which were a useful navigation mark for ships. The current sea defences are maintained by Trinity House and defend the church towers from further erosion.

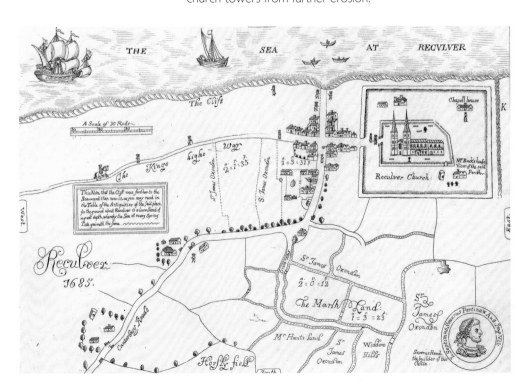

History of Richborough and Reculver

Above: A decorative Iron Age copper alloy mount in the shape of an animal or bird, found at Reculver

Below: A Roman marble bust of Julius Caesar made shortly after his expeditions to Britain in 55 and 54 BC

Facing page: The Emperor Claudius crushing a personification of Britannia, in commemoration of the conquest of AD 43. A mid first-century marble relief from Aphrodisias in modern Turkey

BEFORE ROME

Until the Middle Ages the sites of Richborough and Reculver occupied small promontories on the shores of the Wantsum Channel – a navigable seaway which separated mainland eastern Kent from the Isle of Thanet (see page 7). The Wantsum Channel was probably an important seaway throughout prehistoric times. A sea-going Bronze Age boat found at Dover (now in the town museum) dating to 1550 BC suggests that the people in this part of Britain were familiar with travelling by sea. There were settlements along the Wantsum coast, both on Thanet and the mainland, by the late Bronze and early Iron Ages, about the seventh to sixth centuries BC. Pits, ditches and pottery of this date were found during excavations across the site at Reculver. At Richborough, ditched enclosures and palisade-trenches associated with Iron Age pottery were found across a wide area, suggesting that the site was large and probably important. The indigenous people of Kent at the time of the Roman invasion were organized in a number of petty kingdoms, and Roman material, in particular wine contained in pottery amphorae, had begun to reach the area through trade.

JULIUS CAESAR'S EXPEDITIONS

The first expeditions to Britain by Roman forces were those of Julius Caesar (100–44 BC) in 55 and 54 BC. His campaigns aimed both to punish British tribes that had assisted the Gauls in their fight against Roman occupation, and to enhance his political prestige in Rome. Where Caesar landed his army is not known, though the Richborough and Deal area is a possibility. Caesar's first expedition was a near disaster. His cavalry was delayed by contrary winds, and he landed his infantry on an open beach against stiff resistance from a large force of British tribesmen. His ships were damaged in a storm, and he returned to Gaul with little achieved. His second attempt was more successful, with a larger fleet of ships better adapted for a beach landing. Caesar's forces penetrated inland, crossed the Thames, and forced the submission of the British war leader Cassivellaunus, king of the tribe of the *Catuvellauni*, whose centre was in modern Hertfordshire. Other British chiefs became allies of Rome and diplomatic ties involving the payment of tribute and the exchange of hostages were established.

Above: A copper alloy coin of Cunobelinus, a first-century British king. In the period after Julius Caesar's expeditions, Roman objects began appearing on settlement sites and in the richer graves of British people for whom they were desirable status items, while the design of coinage was influenced by Roman models

Below: This bronze head of the Emperor Claudius was found in the river Alde in Suffolk, and once formed part of a life-sized statue

There were important settlements in east Kent, particularly between AD 20 and 40, following Caesar's expedition. Roman political, economic and cultural influences played a major role in these later Iron Age communities in south-eastern England, owing to the ease of reaching the Continent across the narrow Dover Strait. Two British kingdoms were recognized by Rome as client states, the rulers of which needed the consent of Rome to rule. One was to the north of the Thames, focused in the region that is now Hertfordshire and Essex. This eastern kingdom comprised the tribes of the *Catuvellauni* and the *Trinovantes*. The other was the kingdom of the *Atrebates*, based on the south coast in the area of present-day Sussex and Hampshire. The long-lived and powerful king of the eastern kingdom, Cunobelinus, died between AD 40 and 43, and his succession was disputed, possibly between pro- and anti-Roman factions. At the same time, the king of the southern grouping, Verica, fled to Rome because of internal strife. Perhaps the eastern kingdom was expanding into the territory of its southern rival. Whatever the truth of the situation, it provided a pretext for the Emperor Claudius (10 BC–AD 54) to invade.

THE CLAUDIAN INVASION

Claudius became emperor in AD 41 succeeding his nephew, Caligula. When he was young, he was dismissed by his family as feeble-minded. This certainly helped him survive the power struggles in Rome and in the imperial family during the reigns of Tiberius and Caligula. In the early years of his reign he needed a spectacular demonstration of military prestige in order to underline his legitimacy as emperor and to secure his position.

The invasion of Britain was launched in AD 43. The force comprised four legions (20,000 men), together with a similar force of auxiliaries: a total of 40,000 soldiers, under the command of a senior senator and general, Aulus Plautius. The army gathered on the coast of Gaul, most probably at Boulogne, from where Claudius himself later followed. Sailing was delayed by a mutiny. The soldiers were afraid of crossing the Channel as they believed that the ocean formed the boundary of the world, and that beyond it lay many dangers. A minister of Claudius, Narcissus, quelled the mutiny by haranguing the troops from the general's podium. The fact that Narcissus was an ex-slave appealed to the soldiers' sense of the ridiculous, and this released the tension. The army sailed immediately, crossing in three divisions.

As Roman sources do not mention any place names, the only evidence for the location of their first landing site is the identification at Richborough of a fortified enclosure dating to the conquest period, and the building there, some decades after the invasion, of a great memorial in the form of a triumphal arch (see page 10).

A crossing to Richborough is also the shortest distance from Boulogne, and would have taken advantage of the prevailing winds in the Channel, which are from the south-west.

Many scholars take the view that, because the pretext for invasion was a response to Verica's appeal, it was more likely that the fleet would have landed in his friendly territory on the Solent coast somewhere near Chichester (where there may already have been some low-level Roman military presence). This would have involved a much longer crossing against the prevailing wind. The two ideas are not, however, contradictory.

The Wantsum Channel and the sheltered harbour around Richborough would have made a secure refuge for the fleet. Throughout the age of sail the area of sea off Deal (known as

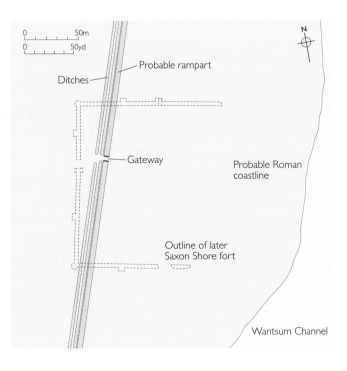

0   50m
0   50yd

N

Probable rampart

Ditches

Gateway

Probable Roman coastline

Outline of later Saxon Shore fort

Wantsum Channel

Above: A Roman galley with a sail and oars. Detail of a mosaic from Hadrumetum, Tunisia

Left: A plan of Richborough in AD 43 showing the location of the Claudian invasion ditches and timber gate in relation to the outline of the later fort and the conjectured Roman coastline

Right: Soldiers disembarking supplies from a ship in a scene from Trajan's Column, Rome, made in the early second century

Below: Bronze statuette found outside the south wall of the fort at Richborough in the 1930s. It represents the deity Bonus Eventus, who was originally an agricultural fertility god, but later became a general symbol of good fortune. He was popular in Britain, and also within the army

the Downs) was a famous anchorage where great numbers of ships would wait for a favourable wind to carry them round the end of Thanet and up to London, or down-Channel to the Atlantic. Although the Wantsum was long gone, the ships took advantage of the shelter offered by the Goodwin Sands. It is likely that the Roman fleet headed across the Channel for a known sheltered harbour at Richborough where a first landfall was made. After this, the fleet might have waited for the wind to come around to carry it along the coast to the Solent.

Upon landing at Richborough, the Romans built a fortified enclosure, consisting of a pair of parallel ditches running for at least 650m from north to south, aligned with the Roman coastline. To the north, the ditches end in an area of marsh. The southern end has been lost in the railway cutting. A single gate has been located, through which passed a road which became Watling Street, the main road to London. Some think that this was one side of a huge fort, big enough to hold the entire invasion force, and that the rest of the fort has been eroded away. Recent excavations, however, suggest that the Roman coast was not far from where the river Stour runs today, beneath the cliff on which the site stands. It is more likely that the fortification was a defence for the invasion beachhead, protecting men, supplies and, crucially, ships.

SUPPLY BASE AND BOOM TOWN

As the end-point of the best sea crossing from Gaul and with a sheltered harbour, Richborough was ideally situated to develop into a major port. Immediately after the initial conquest, the ditches of the beachhead fortification were filled in, and a grid of streets was laid over an area extending well beyond the

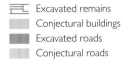

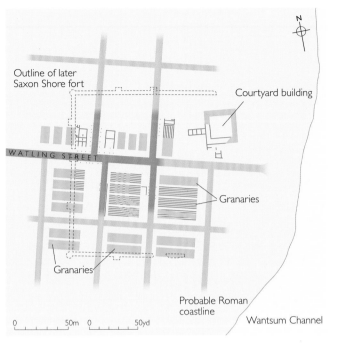

Excavated remains
Conjectural buildings
Excavated roads
Conjectural roads

Outline of later Saxon Shore fort

Courtyard building

WATLING STREET

Granaries

Granaries

Probable Roman coastline

Wantsum Channel

0   50m   0   50yd

walls of the visible fort. These streets lay between large wooden buildings with floors supported on wooden piles. These were store buildings or granaries, probably used to house supplies of grain for the army during the initial phases of conquest. A large courtyard building also in wood may have housed the official in charge of the base.

As the army moved north, it began to supply itself with resources from the newly conquered province and it was not long (probably before AD 70) before the store buildings began to be replaced by small, rectangular, wooden buildings with their short ends fronting onto the streets. These are typical of Roman shops with living quarters behind. They represent the point at which Richborough lost its purely military function and began to develop into a civilian port and town. Some of the

Above: A plan of Richborough in about AD 70 showing the street grid, granaries and courtyard building of the early supply base in relation to the outline of the later fort
Below: Looking west through the west gate of the third-century fort along the line of the Roman road known as Watling Street. The course of Watling Street, marked by the modern bridge and the double row of trees, was established at the time of the Claudian invasion and incorporated into the earliest street grid of the town

Above: A relief from the first century showing a wine shop. A customer in a cloak holds a jug into which the proprietor pours wine through a funnel in the counter

Below: An amphora for Italian wine found in the cellar of one of the buildings of the second-century town

Below right: Map of Richborough in about AD 85 showing the town, complete with shops and a mansio around the monumental arch

store buildings remained, though by now they may have been used for storing goods for export rather than military supplies. The large courtyard building was rebuilt in stone, and may have become a *mansio*, or inn for official travellers. Geophysical survey shows a settlement covering at least 21 ha. Richborough was a boom town, developing as quickly, and at the same time as, the new port and city of London.

THE GATEWAY TO BRITAIN

London was the provincial capital, but Richborough quickly became recognized officially and generally as the gateway to Britain – the *accessus Britanniae* – the main and most important port of entry from the Continent. This status was symbolized in about AD 85 by the building of the arch (see page 10).

For centuries the purpose of its cross-shaped foundation was a puzzle. Excavations produced many pieces of fine white marble cladding and columns from the imperial quarries of Carrara, in Italy. By the time of his death, in 1965, Professor Sir Ian Richmond had realized that the marble fragments and the foundation were remains of a huge, marble-clad monumental arch, about 25m in height, that could only have been built as an imperial project. When the arch was built, the Roman governor of Britain, Agricola (AD 40–93), had just defeated the Caledonians in the battle of *Mons Graupius*, near Inverness. This battle (in AD 83) was thought to have completed the conquest of Britain. The arch was probably built at the order of the Emperor Domitian (r.AD 81–96) to commemorate the completion of the conquest. What better place to do this than where the story began with Claudius' invasion: the port that was still the main access to the province?

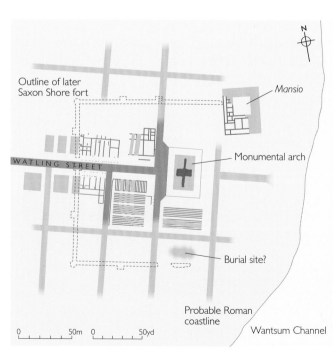

Outline of later Saxon Shore fort

Mansio

WATLING STREET

Monumental arch

Burial site?

Probable Roman coastline

Wantsum Channel

0   50m   0   50yd

Excavated remains
Conjectural buildings
Excavated roads
Conjectural roads

The arch stood at a key symbolic point – the place where the land met the ocean. It was the beginning of the network of roads penetrating into Britain, at the end of Watling Street with which it was purposely aligned. A Roman document known as the Antonine Itinerary, compiled in the third century to describe major routes within the Empire, includes only one Channel crossing: 'from Boulogne of the Gauls to Richborough of the Britains' ('*a Gessoriaco de Gallis Ritupis in portu Britanniam*'). Later generals are recorded as having landed at Richborough, and the name of the site, Rutupiae, was so well known that it was used as a poetic alternative to Britannia by Roman poets.

Monumental Arches

The Richborough arch would have ranked as one of the largest – if not the largest – in the Roman Empire. Free-standing monumental arches were built all over the Empire from the beginning of the imperial period under Emperor Augustus (r.27 BC–AD 14) in the early first century AD. In Rome itself there were more than 50. They commemorated the emperors and their achievements, and were powerful symbols of the imperial personality cult. The Roman writer Pliny the Elder, who died in the eruption of Vesuvius in AD 79, called them 'novel inventions' whose purpose was to 'elevate above all other mortals' the statues of those placed upon them.

Arches were symbolic in several ways. They were erected to commemorate military victories and imperial visits, but they could also mark important boundaries. Most monumental arches had a single opening. Though some had three openings in a line, four-way or *quadrifrons* arches like that at Richborough were rare. The late second-century arch of Septimius Severus at *Leptis Magna* in Libya, which is much smaller than the Richborough arch would have been, and the much later arch of Janus in Rome are the best surviving examples.

At Richborough, this colossal monument would have been unlike anything seen before by the native British population in its size, appearance and the ideas behind it. It must have astonished and awed them.

Left: A coin of Domitian dating to AD 95–6, depicting an arch surmounted by a chariot drawn by elephants. Given that Claudius brought war elephants to Britain, it is tempting to associate this arch with Richborough

Below: The Arch of Titus, in Rome, commissioned by the Emperor Domitian to commemorate the victories of his older brother, the Emperor Titus (r.AD 79–81). The Richborough arch, also built by Domitian, may similarly have marked the defeat of the Caledonians during his reign

THE ROMAN TOWN

The 21 ha town probably developed to its full extent after the completion of the arch. New roads were laid out and stone buildings were constructed. These included a lamp shop and a metal workshop. Stone-built shops appeared around the arch and a new *mansio* complex was erected. This was rebuilt again in about AD 125. The amphitheatre (see page 17) was probably built when the town was at its height. It is set in a high position at the edge of the settlement. Because of what happened in them, amphitheatres symbolized boundaries, between order and chaos, civilization and barbarism, and life and death. The unusual high situation of the amphitheatre and its proximity

to the sea may mean that it formed part of a set of ritual buildings reflecting the boundary between sea and land. To the north of the amphitheatre, and also near the water's edge, was a sanctuary containing at least two stone-built temples.

By the early part of the third century there is evidence that the town was in decline, with buildings and roads going out of use, and burials (which usually took place outside the urban area) encroaching to the south of the monument, within the area of the later Saxon Shore fort. Perhaps the commercial importance of Richborough was being eclipsed by the rise of the port of Dover, though literary evidence shows that the symbolic significance of Richborough remained high.

Above: *A reconstruction of the port town of Richborough at its greatest extent in about AD 120. The drawing is based on the evidence from geophysical surveys and excavation*

Excavated remains
Conjectural buildings
Excavated roads
Conjectural roads

Right: Plan of Richborough in about AD 250. The monumental arch was surrounded by three concentric defensive ditches, which were cut through the stone buildings of the earlier town

Below: A decorative terracotta plaque of a Germanic tribesman dating to about AD 200. Attacks upon the imperial frontiers by Germanic tribes prompted the construction of the system of Saxon Shore forts as early as the later second century

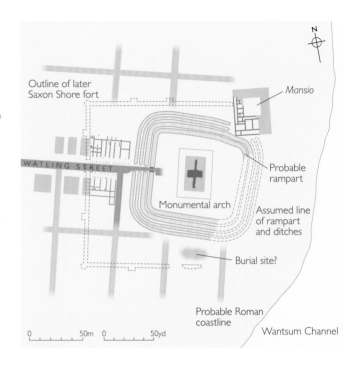

Outline of later Saxon Shore fort

Mansio

WATLING STREET

Probable rampart

Monumental arch

Assumed line of rampart and ditches

Burial site?

Probable Roman coastline

Wantsum Channel

0   50m 0   50yd

THE SAXON SHORE

By the mid third century there were growing problems on the imperial frontiers on the Continent. In 258 and again in 260, the Rhine frontier was breached, and Germanic tribes attacked Gaul. Through the later third century Saxon and Frankish pirates and raiders began to appear in the North Sea.

A scheme of defences around the eastern and southern coast of Britain had begun from as early as the later second century. During the second half of the third century the system developed until by about AD 300 there were 11 forts including Richborough (Rutupiae) and Reculver (Regulbium). The sites were carefully chosen in order to watch and defend estuaries and rivers that might have allowed raiders to penetrate into Britain. These forts are collectively known as the Saxon Shore forts, as nine of them were listed in a late fourth-century document (the *Notitia Dignitatum*) as being under the command of a military officer known as the Count of the Saxon Shore of Britain (*Comes Litoris Saxonici per Britanniam*). Richborough and Reculver operated as a pair to keep watch over the Wantsum Channel. The importance of the Wantsum was not merely as a passage between the mainland and Thanet; the river Stour emptied into the Channel and was navigable at least as far inland as Canterbury (Durovernum).

Reculver was an early element of the Saxon Shore system. Begun by AD 185–200, it was one of three forts constructed to a regular first-century design (see page 21), the others being at Brancaster and Caister, both on the north Norfolk coast. It was garrisoned by the *cohors I Baetasiorum, Civium Romanorum* (the first cohort of Baetasii, Roman citizens), an auxiliary infantry unit from Germany (see page 22).

Left: The inner ditch of the mid third-century fortification around the monumental arch at Richborough slices through one of the earlier stone buildings of the civilian town

Below: The base of the south-west circular corner tower of the late third-century Saxon Shore fort at Richborough. This view gives an impression of the massive solidity of the fort walls

THE FORT AT RICHBOROUGH

A new military phase began at Richborough somewhat later, in the middle of the third century. Three large ditches and an earthen rampart were constructed around the monumental arch. This required the demolition of stone buildings in the *insulae* (town blocks) immediately around the monument, moving people out of their shops and homes. The two outer ditches stopped short of the walls of the *mansio*, which remained in use during this time, possibly acquiring a military function. This work created a military installation with the arch probably becoming a watch- or signal-tower.

The ditches around the arch were filled in at some time shortly after about AD 273 and the construction of the massive walls of the fort began soon after. The requirement for a military post on the site was obviously thought sufficient to justify the complete demolition of the arch, which had stood as a symbol of the entrance to Britain for almost exactly 200 years. Materials from its destruction were reused in the walls of the new fortification, the Italian marble cladding being broken up and burnt to provide lime for the concrete. There are a few places where marble fragments are visible in the core of the fort walls (see page 5).

Archaeological evidence suggests that the new Saxon Shore forts at Dover and Lympne, and probably others, were also built in the mid 270s. All of these new forts were built in the new style of military architecture (see page 21), featuring thick concrete walls and external towers and bastions. Historians generally believe that these impressive forts were built in response to increasing raids by Saxons and Franks, although there are other ideas (see pages 40–41).

CARAUSIUS

In AD 286 Diocletian (c.AD 244–311) became emperor and established a new administrative system known as the Tetrarchy. The Empire was split between west and east, each half being ruled by a senior emperor (or *Augustus*) with a junior colleague (or *Caesar*). The *Augustus* and *Caesar* of the west were Maximian (c.AD 250–310) and Constantius Chlorus (c.AD 250–306). The equivalent positions in the eastern empire were occupied by Diocletian and Galerius (c.AD 260–311). In AD 286 a naval command encompassing the northern coast of Gaul and the coast of Britain was given to an officer named Carausius. His task was to clear the seas of Frankish and Saxon raiders. Following an accusation that he allowed raiders to attack so that he could then intercept them and grab their booty for himself, Carausius fled to Britain and declared himself emperor – a third *Augustus*, equal in status to Diocletian and Maximian. Carausius claimed territory comprising Britain and areas of northern Gaul, including the ports of Boulogne and Calais. Maximian campaigned unsuccessfully against Carausius in AD 288–9. In AD 293, Constantius Chlorus captured Boulogne, and at about the same time Carausius was assassinated by his finance minister, Allectus. The rebel empire continued for a further three years, but in AD 296 Constantius launched a successful reinvasion of Britain, his forces landing in the Solent. Allectus was defeated and killed, and the British provinces were recovered for Rome.

There is archaeological evidence that the Saxon Shore forts at Pevensey and Portchester were built during the reigns of Carausius and Allectus, and some historians have suggested that the whole Saxon Shore system was built as a defence

Above: Carausius minted his own coins bearing propaganda messages. On this silver coin he is depicted alongside the two legitimate Augusti, *Diocletian and Maximian, describing them as his 'brothers' (Carausius et fratres sui)*

Right: A copy of a gold medallion from Arras in France, showing the triumphant Constantius Chlorus arriving in a warship and being welcomed into the city of London after his defeat of Allectus. The inscription celebrates the 'restoration of the eternal light' of Rome

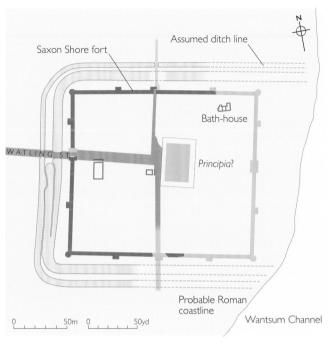

Excavated remains
Conjectural buildings
Excavated roads
Conjectural roads

Left: A plan of Richborough in about AD *280. Little is known about the internal buildings of the fort, but it is thought that the headquarters building (*principia*) probably stood on the site of the demolished triumphal arch*
Below: This stone relief of a goddess dating to the first century was found face-down in the north-west corner of the fort. It is thought to have been reused there as the threshold stone of the late Roman Christian church within the fort

against the possibility of Roman reinvasion. This is not true of Richborough. Carausian coins were found in large numbers in archaeological levels relating to the first occupation of the Saxon Shore fort, but they were absent in the construction layers. This shows that, though the fort was occupied during the reign of Carausius, it was built before he seized power. It is most likely that Richborough and other forts were responses to the threat of raiding. The appointment of Carausius was originally a response to the same problem, so it seems that he inherited an existing defensive system to which he added.

THE FOURTH AND FIFTH CENTURIES

During the fourth century the fort settlement at Reculver declined. In the early part of the century one barrack burned down and was never rebuilt, although wooden buildings may have been constructed within the fort walls. The *Notitia Dignitatum*, the late fourth-century document that records the Saxon Shore command, shows the *cohors I Baetasiorum* still in garrison there.

At Richborough, late third- and fourth-century occupation is difficult to identify in excavation. Like many of the Saxon Shore forts the internal layout is not well understood. The headquarters building (*principia*) is thought to have occupied the position of the great monument, and a small bath-house lay on the site of the former *mansio*. Two other stone buildings dating to this time have been excavated, though their functions are unknown. In the north-west corner of the site a hexagonal tile-built structure was found. This is the font of a late Roman Christian church, and resembles others that have been found in forts on the Continent. It may have occupied a

'[Count Theodosius reached the coast of] Boulogne, from which the spacious land opposite is separated only by a narrow space of a sea wont in turn to swell with dreadful surges and again, without any danger to sailors, to sink to the form of a level plain. From there he quietly crossed the strait and landed at Rutupiae [Richborough], a quiet haven on the opposite coast.' Ammianus Marcellinus, *Res Gestae* xxvii, 8.6

Facing page: An 1850 engraving of an Anglo-Saxon brooch found at Richborough. This spectacular find shows that Richborough remained in occupation after the Roman period. The brooch is held in the World Museum, Liverpool

Above: Detail of a mosaic from Ostia, Italy, showing a Roman ship
Right: A small sample of the many thousands of coins found across the site at Richborough. The vast number of coins to be found here was remarked upon as long ago as 1540, when the antiquarian John Leland noted that 'in going to plough there has ... [been found] more antiquities of Roman money than in any place else of England'

baptistery adjacent or linked to a small timber church built on stone blocks laid on the ground surface. The vast number of fourth-century finds from the site indicates though that the fort was heavily occupied. Excavations within the area of the fort yielded a staggering 43,616 fourth-century coins, and the 63 brooches of the so-called 'crossbow' type are by far the largest number from any site in Britain. Buildings were likely to have been of timber. Their traces were probably missed by the early 20th-century excavators, though hearths and floors were sometimes noted.

At Reculver, occupation appears to have ceased by about AD 375, as very few coins after this date have been found on the site. Why Reculver was abandoned is unknown, but it must have been part of a military reorganization the purpose of which is not understood.

Richborough, meanwhile, continued to be important as the entrance to Britain. In AD 360, the general Lupicinus, *Magister Equitum per Gallias* (Master of the Horse for Gaul), arrived here with troops to campaign against the Picts and Scots in the north. In AD 367 Count Theodosius (d.AD 376), appointed *Comes Britanniarum* or Count of the Britains, landed here with an army to quell the invasions of Picts, Scots, Saxons, Franks and Atacotti known as the 'Great Barbarian Conspiracy'.

The late garrison of Richborough was a detachment of *legio II Augusta* (the second Augustan legion). At Richborough over 20,000 Roman coins from the period AD 395–402 were found scattered in the latest archaeological deposits and in the topsoil. This is more than in the whole of the rest of Britain. It is the last place in the province to which coins were supplied in quantity, and why so many small value coins were lost here remains a mystery, though it must reflect financial activity, possibly as a market centre. A further discovery dating to the late fourth or early fifth century was the burial of a warrior, probably a late Roman auxiliary soldier, carrying Germanic inspired equipment. This may indicate the presence of a cemetery of this period to the north of the fort.

AFTER ROME

A scattering of coins from Richborough dates from the late fifth century to the medieval period, and there is a tradition that St Augustine (d.c.604) landed here at the beginning of his mission to convert the pagan Anglo-Saxons to Christianity in 597 (see below). This tradition was strong in the Middle Ages, when a small chapel dedicated to Augustine was built. There are a few references to the chapel in medieval manuscripts, for instance in 1294 the roof was reportedly in bad condition. When excavated, the chapel was found to be in the centre of a small cemetery and to have had at least three phases of building. The original chapel was rebuilt in the 12th century, and was in continuous use until the 17th century.

Below the fort at Richborough the Wantsum Channel began to silt, becoming partially marshland, and the cliff on which the fort stood eroded. This made the east wall unstable, and it collapsed, sliding down the slope into the mud. The fallen wall was used in the 15th century as a minor waterfront

St Augustine in Kent

In 595, Augustine, prior of a monastery in Rome, was chosen by Pope Gregory the Great (c.540–604) to lead a mission to convert the English to Christianity, beginning with King Ethelbert of Kent (c.560–616). Kent was chosen because of its proximity to Christian Gaul, and also because Ethelbert was married to a Christian – Bertha (c.539–612), daughter of King Charibert of Paris. In 597 Augustine landed and made his way to Ethelbert's court at Canterbury. Bede says he landed on Thanet, but later traditions say it was Richborough. Others say he landed first at Thanet, crossing to Richborough with Ethelbert's permission. In the Middle Ages the association with Richborough was strong. Thus the chapel was dedicated to Augustine, and the reused

lion sculpture at the north gate got the name of 'Queen Bertha's Head'.

King Ethelbert converted to Christianity and allowed the missionaries to preach freely, giving them land to found a monastery outside the walls of Canterbury. Augustine was consecrated bishop of the English and converted many of the king's subjects, including

Left: This decorated initial from an eighth-century copy of Bede's Ecclesiastical History includes a portrait of probably Pope Gregory the Great, although a later writer has identified the figure as St Augustine

thousands during a mass baptism on Christmas Day in 597. Pope Gregory sent more missionaries in 601, together with encouraging letters and gifts for the churches. Roman Catholic bishops were established at London and Rochester in 604, and a school was founded to train Anglo-Saxon priests and missionaries. Augustine died in 604 and was soon revered as a saint. It was King Egbert of Kent (d.673), the great-grandson of Ethelbert, who gave the land at Reculver to Abbot Bassa for the building of the church and monastery in 669.

or dock, associated with stone buildings with tile roofs. It is possible that stone robbed from the fort found its way to the burgeoning town of Sandwich downriver from this dock. At about this time, the authorities of Sandwich gave instructions that wrecks in the channel near Richborough should be removed, as they stopped the water supply into Sandwich Haven. This might have been part of deliberate but illegal attempts to reclaim the channel on the part of those who wished to extend their land holdings.

In the sixth century Reculver became a royal estate. In 669 King Egbert of Kent (d.673) granted land to Abbot Bassa for a monastery. Ten years later, King Hlothere (d.685) made another grant. Abbot Bassa's church was built in the fort enclosure at Reculver, reusing Roman stone and tile. It was dedicated to St Mary the Virgin and consisted of a small nave with an apsidal chancel, separated by stone columns. These now stand in the crypt of Canterbury Cathedral along with fragments of the decorated Anglo-Saxon Reculver Cross, which was still standing in the nave of the church when the antiquarian John Leland visited Reculver in 1540.

The minster church owned trading vessels, and a large number of eighth-century coins found at Reculver suggests it may have been a market, though no post-Roman structures, other than the church, have been located within the fort walls. The church probably suffered during the Viking raids in the ninth century. In 850–51 a Viking army wintered on Thanet, and as late as 1011 Vikings sacked Canterbury. During the ninth century the monastery was abandoned.

THE LATER CHURCH AT RECULVER

In 949 Reculver church was handed to the Archbishopric of
Canterbury. It became a parish church serving a village to the
north which was mostly abandoned by the late 18th century,
and which has now been lost to the sea. The towers that still
stand were added in the 12th century. In 1540 the sea was
still a quarter of a mile away to the north, but rapid erosion
meant that by 1781 the north-west corner of the Roman fort
had fallen away. The eroded material was carried eastwards by
the sea and contributed to the blocking and silting of the
Wantsum Channel. The church became unsafe, and in 1807
the vicar, the Revd Christopher Naylor, persuaded his
parishioners to abandon it. It was demolished with the aid of
gunpowder in 1809, leaving the towers to act as a sea-mark.

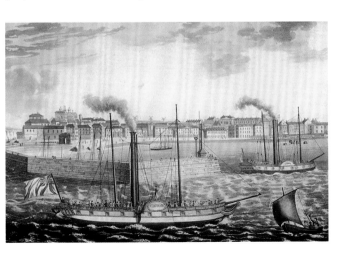

*Above: A watercolour painting of
Reculver church in 1755 by L Sullivan,
looking south-west. The area of the
Roman fort outside the churchyard is
shown under cultivation*

*Left: Some of the stone from the
demolished church at Reculver was
used to build the new parish church
at Hillborough, but 2,000 tons of it
were sold and incorporated into the
construction of Margate Pier, shown
in this painting of 1821 shortly after
its completion*

'I saw it [the tunnel under the monument] by candle within, and there were conies [rabbits]. It was so straight [narrow] that I had no mind to creep far in.'
John Leland, *Itinerary*, 1540

Below: *During his excavations in the Depression years of the 1920s and 1930s, Bushe-Fox recruited a local workforce, including many out-of-work Kent miners, with the specific aim of relieving the high unemployment in the area*

DISCOVERY AND EXPLORATION

In 1540 the antiquary John Leland visited and described both sites. At Reculver his notes on the church and the standing cross are valuable records. At Richborough he saw the walls of the Saxon Shore fort, the cross-shaped foundation of the monument, and the church. These features, apart from the church, were shown on the prospects of the site drawn by the Buck brothers in 1735, and by William Stukeley in 1776. Stukeley also recognized and illustrated the amphitheatre.

Leland noted that 'men [had] sought and digg'd for treasure' around the foundation of the monument, and for the next 400 years people were fascinated by this feature. Recorded excavations took place in 1792, 1826, 1843 and 1865, and there were probably others as well.

Further work on the cross foundation was done as part of the great campaign of excavations led by JP Bushe-Fox for the Society of Antiquaries of London and Ministry of Public Buildings and Works between 1922 and 1938. Bushe-Fox was one of the foremost archaeologists of his time, and was appointed Chief Inspector of Ancient Monuments in 1933. For the time, his techniques were systematic and controlled and he was a pioneer in the study of Romano-British pottery. Using a small railway for spoil disposal, the whole of the area within the walls of the Saxon Shore fort was excavated and laid out much as it appears today. This work forms the basis for current understanding of the site. The work excited great public interest, and in August 1938 there were more than 2,000 visitors.

WARTIME RICHBOROUGH AND RECULVER

During the First World War the area to the east of Richborough was a major temporary port for the embarkation of men and war materials to the Western Front. During the Second World War the site was used again as a transit camp to accommodate Jewish refugees fleeing Nazi-occupied Europe. At the fort itself, trenches and gun pits were dug in connection with the defence of the Battle of Britain fighter base at Manston. The soldiers were instructed to sift the soil to check for Roman coins as they dug. At Reculver meanwhile, the beach was used to test Barnes Wallis's innovative bouncing bomb, used in the famous 'Dam Busters' raid.

Above: Testing Barnes Wallis's bouncing bomb at Reculver beach, on 12 May 1943, less than a week before the bomb was used in a devastating raid on German dams
Below left: Richborough Gantries, a painting of the First World War embarkation harbour by Sir John Lavery, 1917

Above: Refugees at Richborough's 'Kitchener Camp' during the Second World War. According to refugee Herbert Freeden, writing in 1959, '5,000 Jewish men from Germany and Austria, and many of their families, owe their very lives to this forgotten spot'

Above: The solid, circular tower at the south-west corner of the Saxon Shore fort at Richborough

Below: Roman oyster shells discovered during the 2008 excavations at the foot of the embankment on the east side of the Saxon Shore fort at Richborough. The 'Rutupian shore' of Britain was celebrated in Roman literature for the quality of its oysters

MODERN INVESTIGATIONS

The Kent Archaeological Rescue Unit undertook excavations at Reculver between 1959 and 1969, and revealed crucial details of the interior layout and dating of the fort. At Richborough, it had long been recognized that the area within the walls was only part of a much larger settlement. Finds had been recovered from a wide area, and as early as 1887 traces of buildings and roads were seen in the surrounding fields. Remains of a Roman house were found when the railway was built in 1846. Bushe-Fox discovered the temples near the amphitheatre, which had been excavated with trenches in 1859. In 2001 English Heritage carried out aerial photography and geophysical surveys to establish the size of the settlement. The discovery that it was at least 21 ha in extent showed that Richborough had indeed been a flourishing and extensive Roman town. In 2001 and again in 2008 excavations by English Heritage showed that the Roman coastline was not much further away than the modern river course. Further opportunities to explore the hidden histories of these fascinating sites may occur in the future.

As Saxon Shore forts, Richborough and Reculver stand at the very beginning of the military fortification of the south-east coast of England – a story which spans nearly 2,000 years. Many examples of these different fortifications are now in the care of English Heritage.

Martine Sitbon

Alternative Vision

Martine Sitbon: Alternative Vision
© 2016 Rizzoli International Publications, Inc.
300 Park Avenue South, New York, NY 10010
www.rizzoliusa.com

© 2016 Martine Sitbon

Edited by Marc Ascoli and Martine Sitbon

Creative Direction by Marc Ascoli

Texts: © Olivier Saillard, © Angelo Flaccavento, © Frédéric Sanchez,
© Fabrice Paineau, © Nick Knight

Cover: © Mario Sorrenti/Art Partner Licensing

Publisher: Charles Miers
Editorial Direction: Catherine Bonifassi
Graphic Design: Atelier 32, Diego Fellay & Chloé Berthaudin
Production: Alyn Evans
Editor: Daniel Melamud
Copy Editor: Victorine Lamothe-Maurin
Translator: Emma Sroussi

Editorial Coordination:
Cassi Edition, Elsa Whyte

Library of Congress Control Number: 2016940670
ISBN: 9780847849383
2016 2017 2018 2019 / 10 9 8 7 6 5 4 3 2 1
Printed in China

Martine Sitbon

Alternative Vision

Edited by
MARC ASCOLI & MARTINE SITBON

RIZZOLI
NEW YORK

New York Paris London Milan

Photo booth, circa 1980.

FOREWORD

Martine is ambivalent—she is both profound and playful.
Our relationship is a continual exchange; we are exceptionally close.

An incredibly complete woman, Martine has managed to shape her
own world over the years. What is this world like? Shadowy, childlike,
feminine, androgynous, rock, poetic, nonchalant, violent, and elegant,
as though it came from the streets.

It stems from all these contrasts, in a moving field of opposites where
the Parisian spirit flies beyond its boundaries. In this surge
of generosity, Martine enjoys sharing all of her desires with us.
It is an open-ended conversation . . .

MARC ASCOLI

MARTINE (15 ANS) AVEC LES STONES AU
MARQUEE CLUB

TOUT
PETIT (3
MOMO

SES 9 ANIMAUX

MARTINE 4 ANS SUR LA TERRASSE
A CASABLANCA

CRÊPÉE PAR SA SOEUR MARTINE
ARRIVE À PARIS 10 ANS

SA MÈRE A CASABLANCA

*Pretty (and funny!) presentation of my childhood and teenage memories
by Mathias Augustyniak and Michael Amzalag, June 1994.*

Reapplying lipstick in a London taxi.

In the studio in a red sweater at the end of the 1980s.

Four years old in the street in Casablanca.

At the beach.

Roman holiday with my mother, Dina.

On the terrace with my little trench coat.

With my mother and older sister Danièle in the street in Casablanca, dressed identically.

On the beach in Casablanca with my mother and two older sisters.

A few years later, I inherited Danièle's dress.

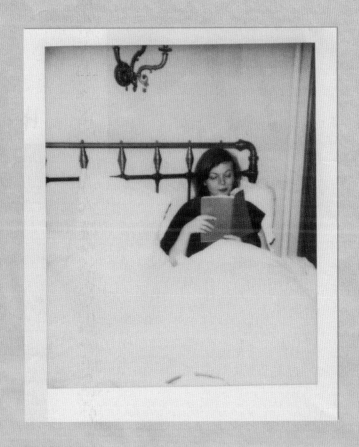

New York, aged seventeen with a curly perm.

The following partial text is visible in the left column:

king speed on a dull
meras were ru
ractured... while
corner.

l entered a private
t new circle of cr
y needed them a
g pop art with
can way of life
nning the melti
become the ex
Inevitable (E.P.I.
young bodies,
He vampirized
rs, sucking their
cial to both par
s the thin, slight
elor Paul Morris
ungs and also th
d pop artist.
bulous and fun,
udgement. It the
surd piece of pl
rtions, that was a
the circumstan
f plastic to do s
surprising in its
st the system. B
y would become
direct manner
uresque echoes
anthers and ant
nostalgia toda
certainty, still t
ing the present.
d subject, its ex
r *The Velvet U
under his patron

The ultimate Velvet
Underground collector's
item, their very limited
pressing first single
with picture sleeve (Phil
Milstein collection)

A teenager dreaming about The Velvet Underground.

SIT...

The recent French ... new names to th... world. AMANDA

Photograph by NICK KNIGHT

C'EST SITBON

The recent French collections have brought new names to the attention of the fashion world. AMANDA GRIEVE meets one of them

Photograph by NICK KNIGHT

...ghter who ...s most ...hell, her ...here

Martine Sitbon (above) ...s but nobody a frogged frock coat ... seen anything. whimsical drawin ...ce left, I rang the ... asked if they ... the window as ...ssible. They said ...not themselves as ...ld board the win-...ed out for that, ...same day. By ... me had been, so I ...ouncil again. This ...ourse...pair it the same ...mad. I did not ...the flat on my ...with a broken ...uld not have

Photograph by NICK KNIGHT

C'EST SITBON

The recent French collections have brought new names to the attention of the fashion world. AMANDA GRIEVE meets one of them

C'EST SITBON

The recent French collections have brought new names to the attention of the fashion world. AMANDA GRIEVE meets one of them

...ove) in
...t; her
...(right)

...unding in the principles of the
...ensive Parisian design school
...i, where spirit and imagina-
...ch as aptitude and business
...ht us not to lose sight of
... in our own ideas which, as
... design, began to recur as
...nages which sell. This, after
...f good design. It cannot be

...Berçot eager to test her
... limit, by accepting the
... a competitive sportswear
...ompany "So". Two years
... determination to design
...ving won the confidence
...oduced the first designs

under her own name in 1984. "I had learned my grammar, now I could begin to write a poem. All my clothes have this classical construction beneath their frivolity."

Her skill and ingenuity and the encouragement of Marc Ascoli, artistic director for Sitbon and stylist for Yohji Yamamoto, propelled her through two formative collections whose success led to her first catwalk show last October.

The most telling clothes from her winter collection are the simplest — scarlet velvet smock dresses; double-tiered frocks beneath short bolero jackets; little A-line coats — where her gift for generating colour and mood left one feeling here was just the right amount of theory applied to form.

The rather arch gaiety of her clothes is in line with the work of both Vivienne Westwood and Jean Paul Gaultier, yet her collection has all the poise of an elegant Parisienne.

PREVIOUS PAGES · Martine photographed by Nick Knight in *The Independent*, 1987.
ABOVE · Portrait of Martine Sitbon by Javier Vallhonrat at the end of the 1980s.

MARTINE SITBON, OF DRESSES & DREAMS

Olivier Saillard

Certain artists write their works on white pages made black by organized ink. Others set up easels and stretch a canvas over a frame instead. Painters define lines and curves with a stroke of their brush, inventing arabesques that will one day be their signatures as well as their daily journal. Yet others mold a sculptor's destiny in clay or bronze. All of these artists have gained legitimacy and official recognition in the history of art. Couturiers and fashion designers are often dismissed from books that teach the art of self-expression via a pen, a tool, or a tube of color. Nothing is less mysterious however, than cutting a pattern, choosing a fabric, or judging tone and nuance. This encounter with the ephemeral—considered frivolous by some—is a combination of myriad skills. One must be a painter to blend different hues of velvet or mousseline. One must be a sculptor to assemble a sleeve or assess the volume of a dress. And one must be a poet so that every piece of clothing might tell a story beyond the linings and pockets that entertain cloakrooms.

Since the mid-1980s, Martine Sitbon has embodied her profession through the couturier's scissors, the artist's overalls, and the poet's scribblings. She added additional territory with the music that guides her needles and maps out the collections like scales. From 1985 onward, every six months, Sitbon would woo the next season with sewn or draped designs. Runway shows followed one another like the isolated chapters of an essay whose contents escaped the designers themselves. Imagining that they renew forms and ideas from spring through winter, the greatest of them prove, on the contrary, that their influence lies only in the continuity of their style. Enigmatically at first and then lucidly, regardless of the item of clothing chosen, they can turn their hand to a shoulder, a hem, or a collar. This technical vocabulary stemming from pattern-making and cutting becomes a composition that they like to corrupt, the better to subjugate it. Sitbon's obsessions led her to focus on characteristic clothing, materials, and colors. In an unconventional encyclopedia of fashion, the designer would hold the title of "couturier of riding coats and dresses." Those were the two great tomes that she endeavored to illustrate for over twenty years.

To select the ten most representative collections of Martine Sitbon's work, one must view each season's lookbook. These little compilations of photos from the catwalks effortlessly pluck the thirty to fifty looks that articulate the stanzas of a poetic show. In this extensive, far-reaching topography of sweaters and shirts, of long and short dresses, and of men's suits usurped for women, there lies a surprising coherence, as though Sitbon had never doubted her aesthetic ambitions. For all that, her designs are never arrogant or self-assured. Tactfully, sometimes hesitantly, and always gently, her velvet and gabardine designs knock rather than force their way in. Let there be no mistake though, there is gravitas and darkness in Sitbon's work. For though the designer likes to tell stories, they are less about waking the young girl within each woman than about revealing the worries of the adolescent girl, of whom she will never lose sight. Colors are deep or washed-out, while prints are disquieting shadows, and flowers are on the verge of parting with life.

Upon this fragile equilibrium, which ranges from the pretty to the alarming, Martine Sitbon invented her finest collections. Two periods characterize the designer's journey. The first, from 1985 to 1994, explores the multiple possibilities of men's dandy suits, which Sitbon adapted for the feminine wardrobe. The second period, from 1994 to 2014, saw the birth of a subtle colorist, tasteful and defiant in her search for new materials and on which she remains a much-appreciated authority.

For this book, the designer herself agreed to choose the ten collections that tell her story. The first among them, Autumn/Winter 1986–1987, celebrates the men's jacket, which is deconstructed by Sitbon. She lengthened its tails with free-flowing panels, combined broad stripes with skater skirts, and lacerated dresses, proving, with her second collection, her mastery of asymmetry. Long coats decorated with fur and stark, fitted jackets over endless skirts structured the Autumn/Winter 1993–1994[I] collection. The sultry show was punctuated by the appearance of faded flowers worn as necklaces by melancholy girls. For Spring/Summer 1994,[II] the men's suit was still dominant, countered by pajamas for evening and day. Long dresses that were light and fluid made regular appearances.

A voluntarily haphazard wardrobe established the random element of a tartan coat over a printed dress: For Autumn/Winter 1996–1997, [III] the first dresses in *dévoré* velvet and mousseline appeared. The flowers on them were skillfully ragged, while tone-on-tone stripes exuded the charm of cut stems.

The search for fabrics, whose properties Martine Sitbon used to accentuate a relief or bring out a pattern, culminated in the Autumn/Winter 1997–1998 [IV] collection. Dresses were like snapshots of forest undergrowth at twilight. Disquieting motifs, such as leaves and branches in red and black, formed one of the designer's most beautiful collections. For Spring/Summer 1998,[V] Sitbon contradicted this black romanticism with a conceptual show that played on simple constructions and solid colors without departing from a juxtaposition of contrasting materials. Autumn/Winter 1998–1999[VI] sounded a tribute to Rothko. Handkerchief dresses appeared like painted works of art. Geometrical motifs were immersed in the small curls of a fabric that alternated with fluid mousseline. Skirts and dresses were like crumpled paper in Autumn/Winter 1999–2000.[VII] Pleated, painted, tortured, and finished with ribbons, the designs showed a rare poetry, dazzling like a rough draft saved from oblivion. Fresh dresses, overalls, and slips reconstructed the Spring/Summer 2002[VIII] collection that some were to interpret as a soothing balm in a period of turmoil where the future seemed bleak. Dresses that had something of the 1920s and 1930s about them were the basis for Sitbon's Autumn/Winter 2002–2003[IX] collection. She partially discolored fabrics, destroyed the bottoms of dresses, and dipped flowers in ominous water. Autumn/Winter 2003–2004[X] stood out for its multiple uses of stripes and for its racy cutouts. Autumn/Winter 2004–2005[XI] combined, in truly graceful style, paragraph dresses held up by a strap. The three-colored outfits seemed to be linked by their fragile fabrics and cut. Hitched up, draped, and complete in their incompleteness, the dresses, which look like they're about to slip off, are some of Sitbon's most beautiful. From 2011 onward, when the designer signed and set up under the Rue du Mail label, there are three collections that really stand out: Autumn/Winter 2011–2012, Spring/Summer 2012, and Spring/Summer 2013 faithfully sum up the spirit of her designs at the time. Using simple shapes, they pursued the decorative work (relief, embroidery, drawing, and cutouts) that has always been characteristic of Sitbon's pieces. Dazzling colors do not mask a genuine need to forego trends in order to concentrate on the use of fabrics, of which Sitbon is the masterful tailor.

In spite of frequent shows, changing ideas, and the over-production of fashion designs that the discipline entails, a couturier is often remembered for one piece of clothing. Mademoiselle Chanel created the Little Black Dress and then the suit. Dior invented the suit with *basques*. Balenciaga is *the* couturier of dresses. Yamamoto is a master of coats, Alaïa of sheath dresses and jackets, and so on.

The history of fashion can see a pleasing reflection in these pictograms that sum up different eras. They portray the very couturiers who brought them to life on paper, and then in yards of fabric. There was an ambiguity about Martine Sitbon, who first epitomized fitted coats, and then dresses. In this way she espoused the extremities of a wardrobe of opposite nomenclatures. From masculine attire she borrowed shoulders while restoring curves to women. A couturier fantasizes about his creations. He imagines women that are not real, but whom his clients will covet nonetheless. A designer acts differently. She dreams up a collection rather than inventing it. This natural relation to the body and to women creates closeness, and keeps a poetic dialogue open that belongs only to them. Of this, Martine Sitbon is the archetype. Her biography is cut from masculine, pinstripe fabric, from *dévoré* velvet and torn mousseline. Her colors—both tender and dark—tell of her obsessions: those of a woman who sees the adolescent world perish, but remains faithful to the constructed ideals of this age. This *entredeux*, which says everything about Sitbon's fashion, is the signature of her finest collections. When her clothes seem to disappear, perish, and give up like the end of a day, when they are the promise of a night without end, Sitbon no longer belongs only to the ephemeral world of fashion. She has joined the imaginative ranks of great artists.

28

I

II

III

AUTUMN
WINTER
1997-1998

IV

SPRING
SUMMER
1998

V

AUTUMN
WINTER
1993–1994

SPRING
SUMMER
1994

AUTUMN
WINTER
1996–1997

29

AUTUMN
WINTER
1998–1999

VI

AUTUMN
WINTER
1999–2000

VII

30

VIII

IX

AUTUMN
WINTER
2003–2004

X

SPRING
SUMMER
2002

 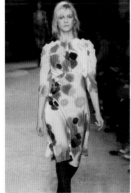

AUTUMN
WINTER
2002-2003

XI

AUTUMN
WINTER
2004-2005

*Personal Polaroid—me and
Kirsten Owen.*

Dear Mark
merci pour les
plus ~~belle~~ les
plus important et
les plus drôle de
memoires de mon
carrer love Kirsten

33

Autumn/Winter 1987–1988 catalog—photographer Javier Vallhonrat, model Kirsten Owen.

MARTINE & MOI, POETICALLY PUNKS

Angelo Flaccavento

D'abord, dear reader, the captatio benevolentiae: These notes will be personal. Utterly, unremittingly personal, and hence a bit disorderly in a spontaneous kind of way. As I face this blank page trying to make sense of the flood of feelings that keep floating in my mind while thinking of Martine Sitbon's work, I welcome the idea that my logical self, maybe, is not the right persona to delve into it, this time at least, if not permanently, in order to satisfy my writing duties. Passion, after all, demands surrender: It defies the rational and urges to embrace the emotional, the contradictory, the glaringly irrational. The chaotic, even. Passion defies explanation: Taste, which is its spark, is certainly a cultural construct, but the seed it stems from is somehow innate, and thus ultimately inexplicable.

I must confess that I have a passion for Martine Sitbon. A deep one that harks back to the exciting afternoons spent flipping through magazines as a provincial child eager to discover new, imagined worlds and escape reality. I've always been an architect of fantastic, never-to-happen situations, and found quite early in my life that the pages of fashion magazines were a wonderful door to other dimensions. Reality is the product of the imagination, after all. Isn't it? My passion for Martine started during those fantasized travels that made my afternoons quite enjoyable, so much so that it somehow became integral to my love for fashion as a whole. I was taken by fashion because it looked essentially like an ever-evolving tool for self-expression. Albeit this was all happening in the thick of the 1980s, when flash, cash, and status ruled. Style as social discourse and never-ending exercise in the aesthetic construction of the public self was what I related to. It was poetic stuff to me, and Martine was right there, showing me the way. She had the words I was looking for, and spoke them in ways that struck a cord within me. There was a suffused sense of romanticism, for a start, matched with a non-precious brand of opulence. Her creations seemed to belong to another world—one of exoticism, glaring lights, and decadent sophistication. Yet, below the hazy, glittery, and psychedelic halos of Nick Knight and Javier Vallhonrat's shots you could distinctly perceive something strict, graphic, a tougher sensibility. Martine's world was full of sultry beauties clad in tailcoats and jabots, wrapped in frills, and mantled in velvets. But her lovely creatures were not frail and fragile. They also looked ready to roll in the mud—the metaphorical mud of metropolitan life, that is. They were of the smoky-eyed, dark, and mysterious Marianne Faithfull kind, not of the sugary, escapist Marie Antoinette variety. The contrast was electrifying. It all looked oh-so-frivolous to me but so lively, bohemian, magnetic.

Forgive me if I am going astray, but the psychedelic fantasies I am recalling along these lines are still with me after so many years—chaotic, touching, and untouched. Should I sum up the Martine Sitbon oeuvre, in fact, I'd do so with a cut-up of feelings and visions.
Here is the tactile yet immediate intricacy of a *dévoré* surface swarming in crisp art nouveau patterns. There is the coiling calligraphy of contrast piping drawing swirling lines allover mannishly romantic tailoring. Here, again, is the metallic luminosity of glitter and the flimsy consistence of transparent man-made fabric. There is a collage of traveling references rendered so light and even as to transcend easy, literal references.
Here is Kristen McMenamy absent-minded on a swing with her Candy Candy locks and diamanté shoes. There is Kirsten Owen, curly hair

and starry makeup like a disco diva, looking straight into the camera while holding a glistening cherry with her glossy lips. These are the images that drew me in, locking forever in my imagination. These are the images that are still with me, twenty or more years later.

But there was also something more tangible to the Sitbon infatuation. Martine Sitbon welcomed me into her decadent world by way of piping, quite literally. Yes, piping: the contrasting silk cord she was using so much at the beginning of her career. I have vivid memories of visiting her Milan showroom on Via Cappuccini, barely aged twelve, with my aunt Tina as she was seeking new stuff for her esoteric boutique in our small hometown of Ragusa. In those rooms I had the revelation of those Sergeant Pepper suits covered in piping. Aunt Tina did not end up buying the collection— she deemed it too outré for her clientele— but I was bewildered. Martine showed me that a decorative approach to style matters does not necessarily call for a rococo outcome. In fact, she was rather rock-oco.

I have been following Martine's path ever since, seeing the spores of her sophisticated thinking touch the farthest fashion lands, morph into something as diverse as the poisonous creatures of Julie Verhoeven or the collage of textures and references that is integral to the Miu Miu lexicon. I have seen her work become edgier and more intoxicating in the '90s and then regain a romantic sensuality with the Rue du Mail installment, when dresses became her pièce de résistance and her aesthetic delved deeply into a kind of pell-mell decadence.

While being a fantastic character-maker, Martine has always struck me for her unique sensibility with fabric, for her sense of color, decoration, and texture. She is a storyteller of the *dévoré*, a poet of the ruffle, an aphorist of dense beading, a haiku-ist of the jet bead, a singer of the glittery. She can transport you on a far-flung journey just by mixing two silks of different weight, or by juxtaposing colors you never thought could go together. Her soul is lyrical but her way with things is never sugary. Her love for intricacy hides a surprising Cartesian lucidity.

This has always been my fantasy about her. Until, one day, I met the real Martine and her husband, Marc, for an intimate, lovely dinner in a crazy Japanese place, Chez Miki, at a stone's throw from their house and my Parisian hotel. This was my first meeting with my heroine, and I was quite tense, honestly. Tension vanished right away. I immediately had the feeling of having found a kindred soul: Here she was, a bit

shy, shielding her boiling personality behind a composed, impeccable demeanor. I immediately thought we were similar. In the silly realm of contemporary social networks, I pride myself of the title, or nom de guerre, of poetically punk. Martine, for me, is poetically punk too, even though she's maybe into another fantasy: the bohemian rock shenanigans that preceded punk by a decade. She's deeply, undoubtedly feminine in her gaze, yet she has a gentle flair for random slash 'n burn. Punk is a state of mind, after all, not a safety pin nor a pair of bondage trousers. It's about an aversion to norms and Dadaist creative anarchy, and Martine surely has both.

In my fantasies, I nurture the desire of a trip—a brief, illuminating one—inside Martine's head, just to see what happens in there. Arianna gave her lover, Theseus, a woolen thread to help him find his way back from the treacherous minotaur's labyrinth. He succeeded. As for me, I could use some silk piping to complete my duties, even though I am sure I'd love to get lost in what to me looks like a glittery, enchanted wonderland crowded with wonderfully stylish creatures. I'm sure I would drop the piping tape at some point and just surrender to Martine's own brand of psychedelia. That night, during our dinner, speaking a very "Sitbon" mixture of broken French, broken Italian, and broken

English—in the sense of very mixed up yet also very effortless—I mentioned the Via Cappuccini episode, and she laughed. Not even in my wildest dreams would I have dared to imagine that the hypnotic spell of those swirls could lead me, years later, to the author herself. Yet it happened, and somehow it closed the circle only to leave it open for further developments. This text, for instance.

So, dear reader, my journey ends here, but maybe this is just a point of departure for another trip. I wish these words were as hazy and haloed as my feelings. Please, imagine my thoughts as if they were written in silky treads, piping ribbons, and jet beads. Close your eyes.

39

41

ABOVE AND OPPOSITE · Spring/Summer 1986—photographer Javier Vallhonrat, model Susie Bick.

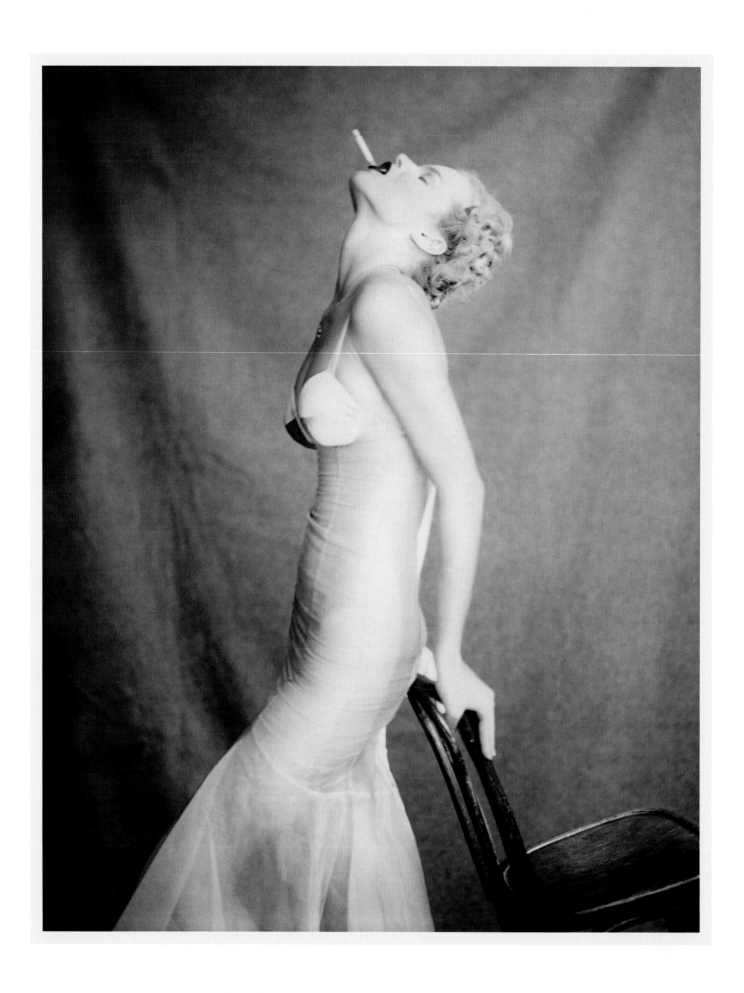

42

ABOVE · Spring/Summer 1993—photographer Paolo Roversi, model Eva Herzigova.
OPPOSITE · Autumn/Winter 1993-1994—photographer Paolo Roversi, model Helena Christensen.

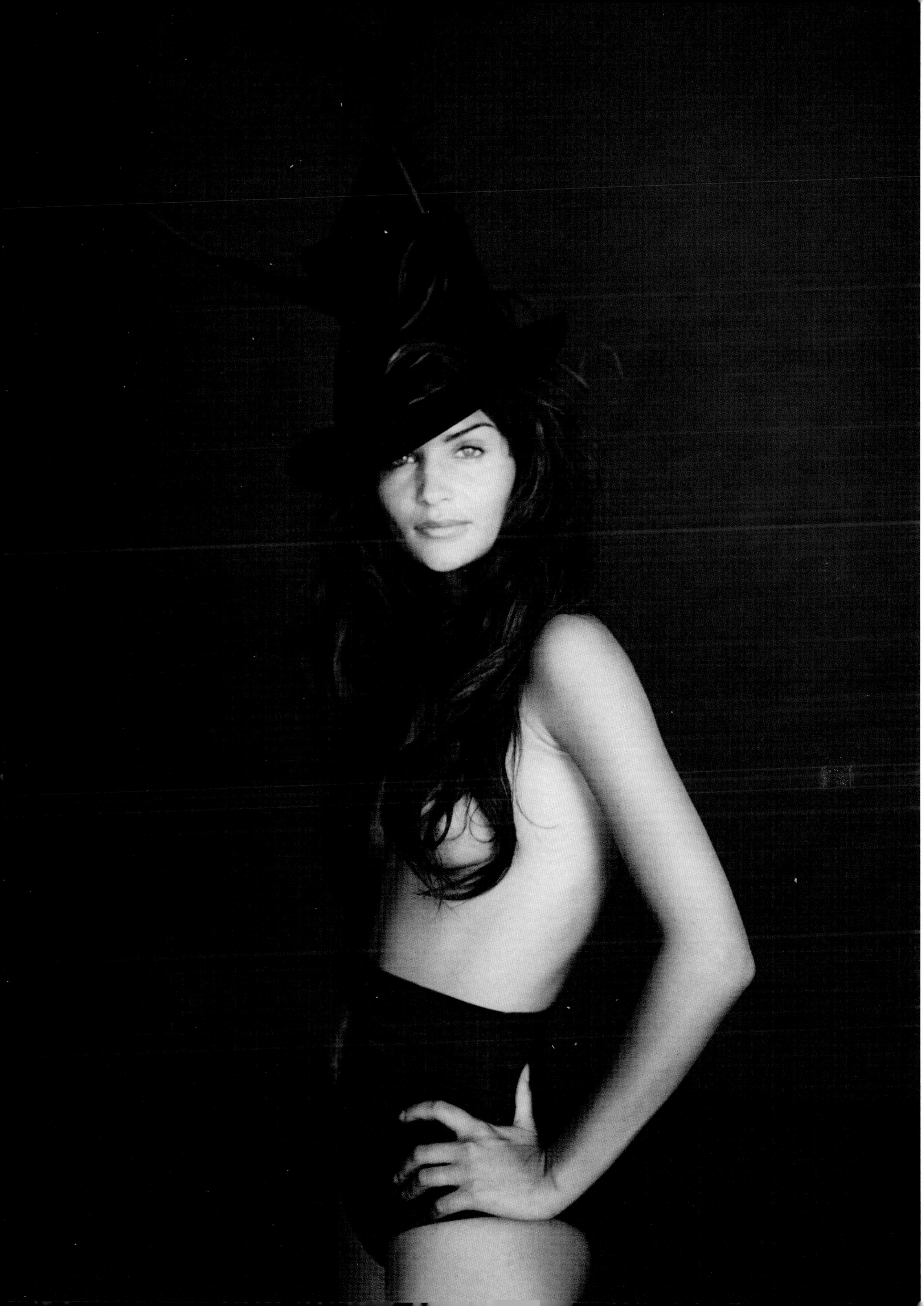

44

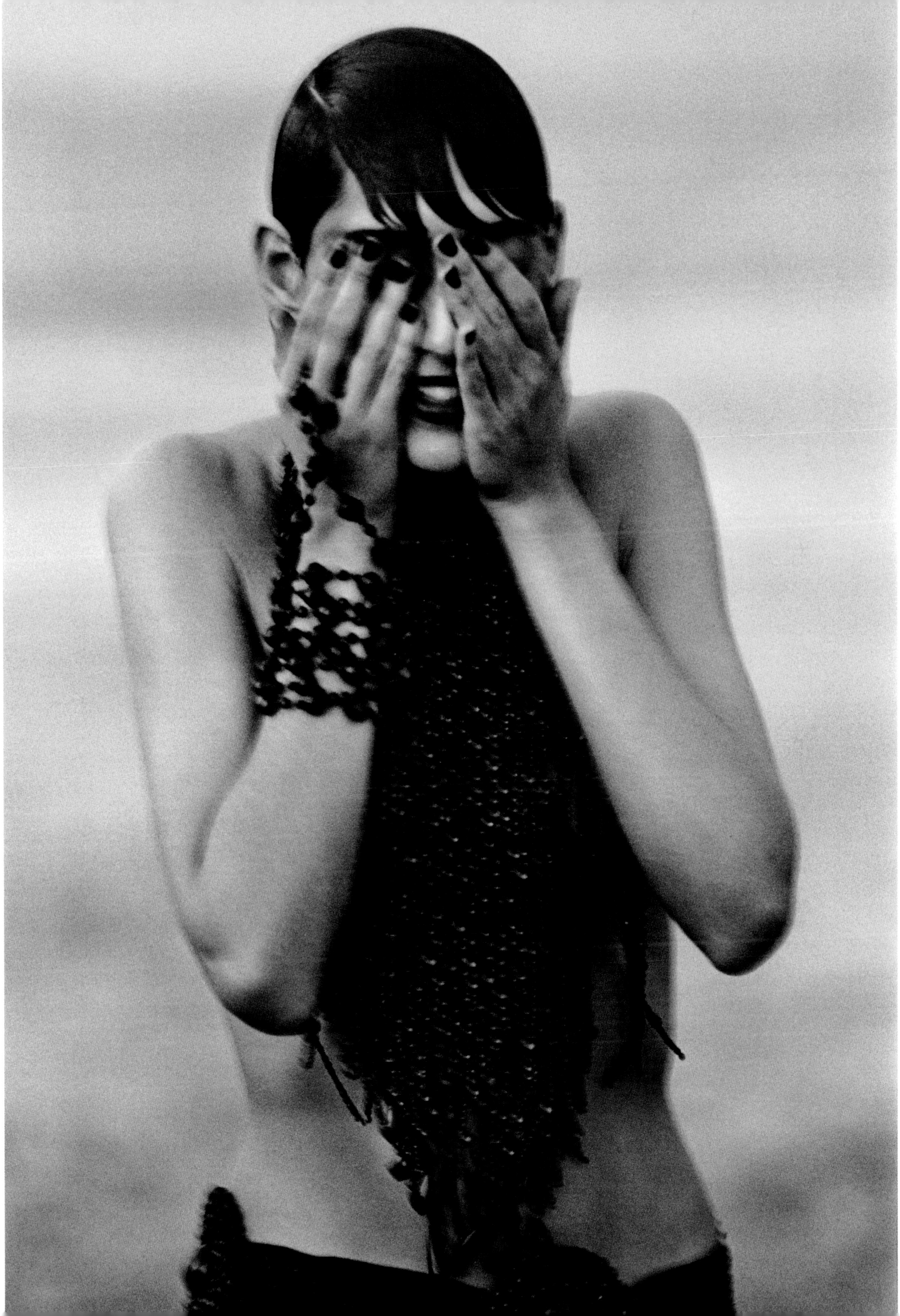

48

PREVIOUS PAGES
(46) · Spring/Summer 1993—photographer Peter Lindbergh, models Kristen McMenamy and Helena Christensen.
(47) · Spring/Summer 1993—photographer Peter Lindbergh.
OPPOSITE · Autumn/Winter 1993-1994—photographer Mario Testino, model Kristen McMenamy.
FOLLOWING PAGES
(50) · Autumn/Winter 1993-1994—photographer Mario Sorrenti, model Kate Moss.
(51) · Autumn/Winter 1993-1994—photographer Satoshi Saikusa.

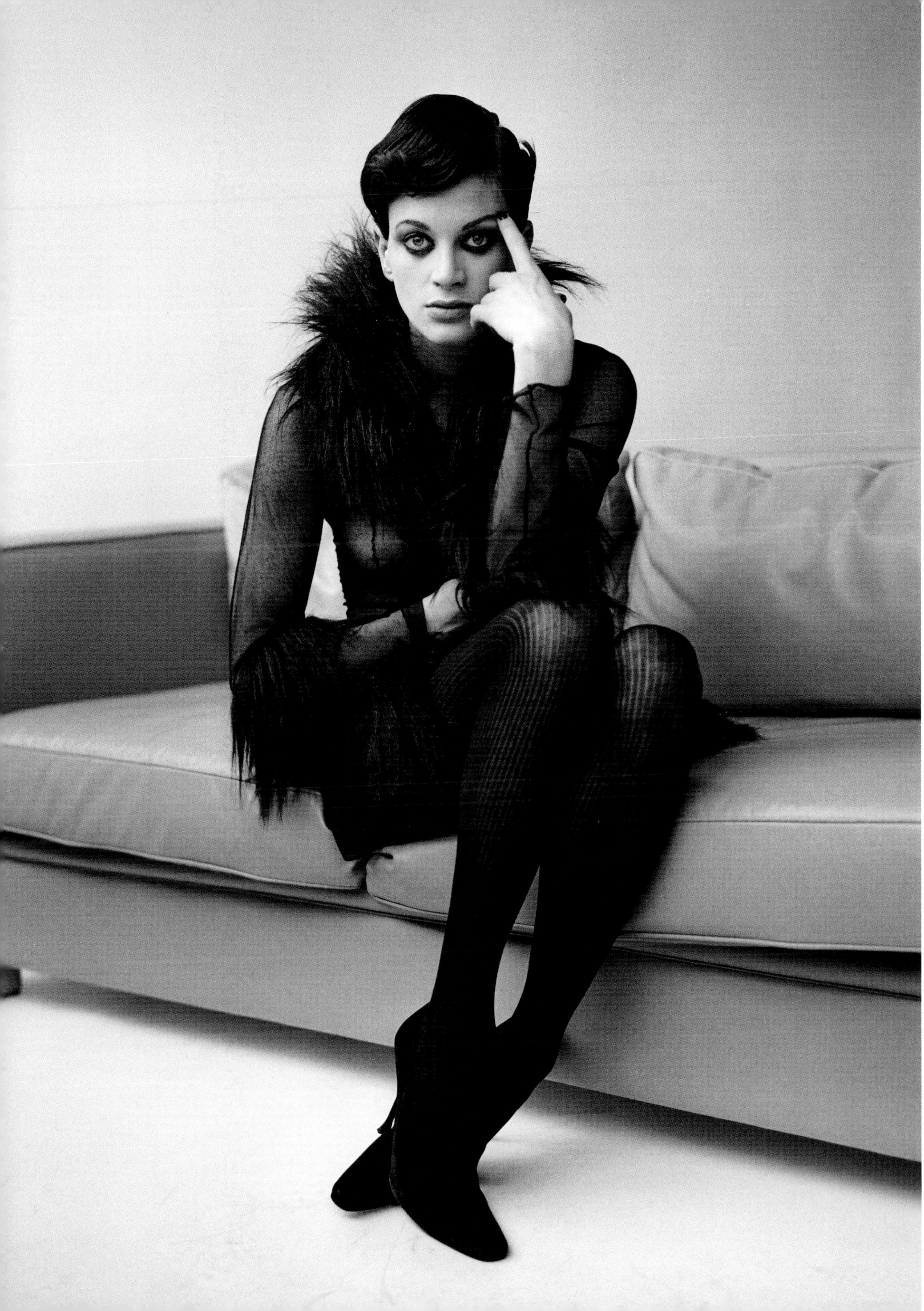

50

PREVIOUS PAGES
(52) · Autumn/Winter 1989–1990 catalog—photographer Javier Vallhonrat, model Amanda Cazalet.
(53) · Autumn/Winter 1989–1990 catalog—photographer Javier Vallhonrat, model Kirsten Owen.
OPPOSITE · Autumn/Winter 1989–1990—photographer Peter Lindbergh.

56

ABOVE AND OPPOSITE · Autumn/Winter 1989–1990 catalog—photographer Javier Vallhonrat.

These drawings and inspirations are part of Julien D'ys's astonishing
notebooks for my "Dandy" collection.

61

OPPOSITE · Martine's personal notebook for the Autumn/Winter 1993–1994 runway show—models Emma Balfour and Rie Rasmussen,
hair by Julien d'Ys, makeup by Stéphane Marais.
ABOVE · Kirsten Owen in Chloé by Martine Sitbon, photographed by Javier Vallhonrat for Italian *Vogue*.

Kirsten Owen in Chloé by Martine Sitbon, photographed by Javier Vallhonrat for Italian *Vogue*.

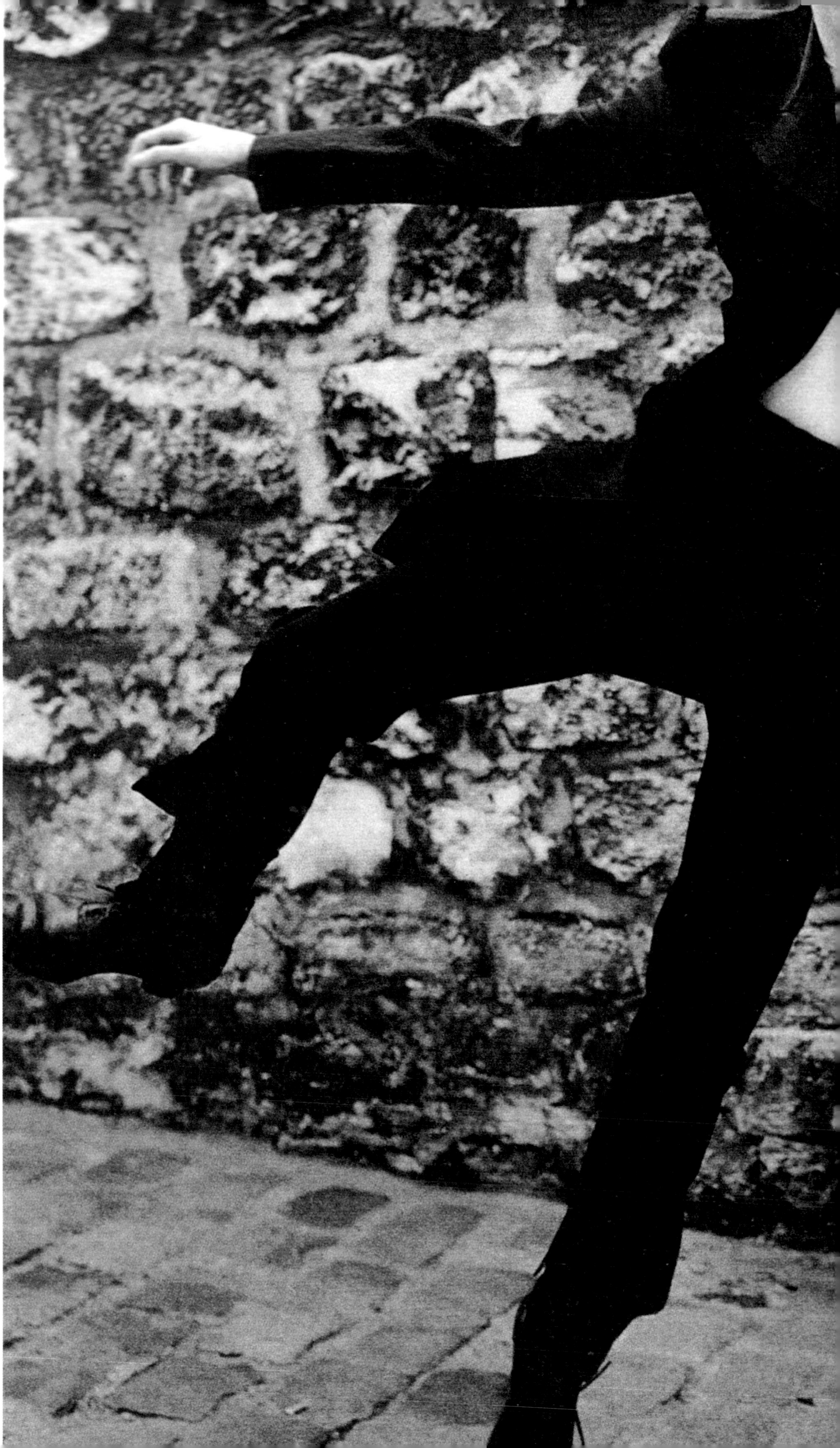

66

MARTINE SITBON, DANDY DOLL →

PASSANT DU DANDYSME ROCK À L'ANGÉLISME
POUDRÉ D'EFFETS PERVERS, MARTINE SITBON
TROUBLE ET ENCHANTE. DOUBLE LECTURE AU FOND DU
MIROIR

ÇA N
cultiv
poupé
au ma
intell
sous-
"Elle
Puces
Mari
gardi
blond
elle é
très
"mai
Rêve
déjà
bulle
des p
dans
En fa
sont
aux c
"à pr
et Ch
gran
l'enf
chale
je le
l'esp
et in
Paris
sa pe
Dans
se sh
et Ri
balay
ingé
sur s
cherc
Epoc
Mart
Porte
la me
de D
A ell
en ve
Perm
aux
quan
je ca
C'est
le pla
peu d
le co
vrai
d'int
deux
l'étra
à Ne
à me
série
Gabr
agre
drôle
ang
Dès
troul

73

OPPOSITE AND PREVIOUS PAGES · Autumn/Winter 1990–1991 catalog—photographer Nick Knight.
ABOVE · Spring/Summer 1990 catalog—photographer Nick Knight.

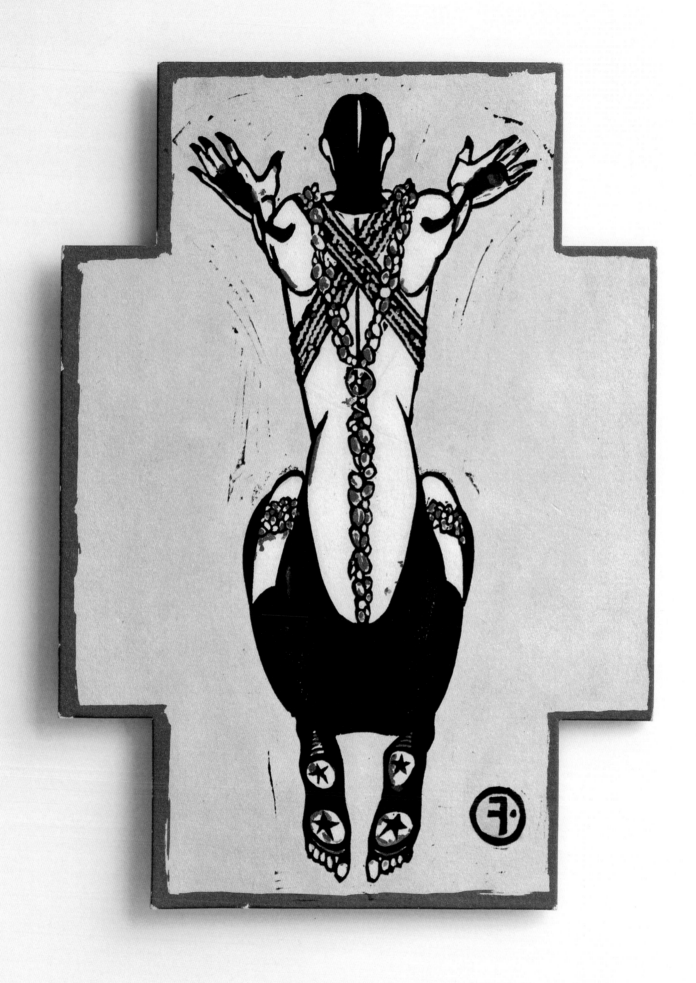

light's Martine Sitbon catalogue cover: not exactly 'dangerous' — even if it manages to upset certain art directors

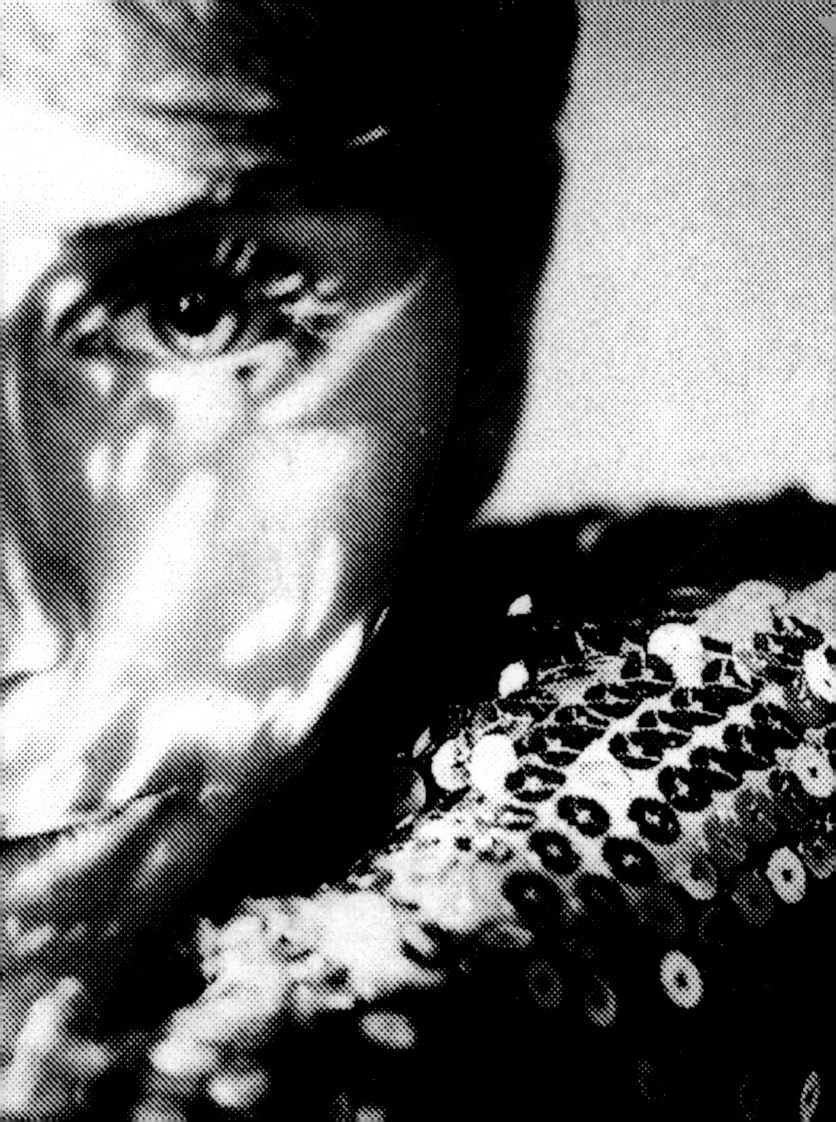

80

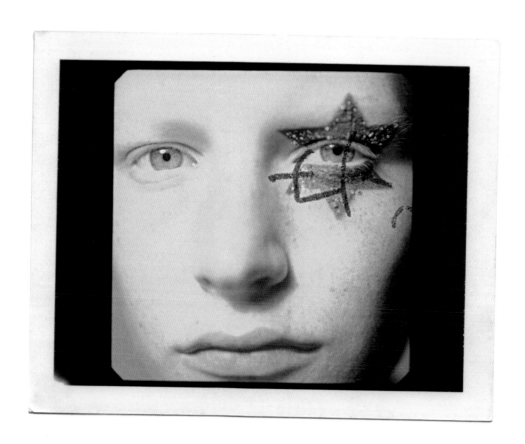

PREVIOUS PAGES · Spring/Summer 1989—photographer Javier Vallhonrat, model Mathilde.
ABOVE · Polaroids from a Nick Knight shoot.
OPPOSITE · Autumn/Winter 1991-1992—photographer Nick Knight, model Kirsten Owen.
FOLLOWING PAGES (82-85) · Autumn/Winter 1991-1992—photographer Nick Knight, model Kristen McMenamy.

85

*The making-of photos from the same shoot
with Craig McDean, who was then
Nick Knight's assistant.*

Kirsten Owen was a favorite model of Marc Ascoli and Martine Sitbon, and a favorite model of mine. She seems to embody that sort of odd, difficult world that Marc likes where the girls aren't overtly sexy. They're more like something from a fairy tale. Martine is very much like that also—there's a lot of childhood in her work and a lot of references to teenage girls as well. The hair reference for this shot was Jane Campion's film *An Angel at My Table*. The whole shoot looked at nursery rhymes—Martine always showed me really lovely books on toys and that kind of thing. But then conversely the New York punk scene also fascinated her.

I liked working with her because her dresses were incredible—they were beautiful to photograph and they conjured up exciting imagery. When you're photographing somebody's clothes, you want them to be providing stories. I always think the narrative in fashion should be in the clothes. With some clothes, it's very hard to get the narrative out, but other clothes immediately give references—that's the thing Martine's always did. The models look fantastic in them and they were always inspired when wearing them— all the models wanted to be in Martine's shows, it really felt like you were part of a wonderful gang. You could say it was *Alice in Wonderland* meets The Velvet Underground. I think a lot of the models got off on that and

enjoyed that—it was about being able to have the freedom of childhood and the naiveté of being a child, but with the deviance of teenagehood.

Martine and Marc also loved to experiment. For the first catalog we did for Martine we used a process where we put a transparency film into a negative developer. It almost messes up the ability of the film to see certain colors—so you could print the model's skin jet-black, even if the model was pale as a lily. We played a lot with that. We could make someone like Kirsten Owen, who was a very very fair-skinned girl, completely jet-black. Martine was very good at accepting those kind of big jumps in aesthetics. Martine was always willing to move things forward and not be scared. So I always wanted to work with her, firstly because of the clothes and the world that she created, but also because she was very open to new imagery and wanted to do things that looked different to the mainstream.

NICK KNIGHT

PREVIOUS PAGES (88-89, 91) · Autumn/Winter 1991-1992—photographer Nick Knight, model Kirsten Owen.
ABOVE · Invitation to the Autumn/Winter 1992-1993 runway show, concept and illustration.
OPPOSITE · Spring/Summer 1994—photographer Paolo Roversi, model Stella Tennant.

Spring/Summer 1994—photographer Paolo Roversi, model Stella Tennant.

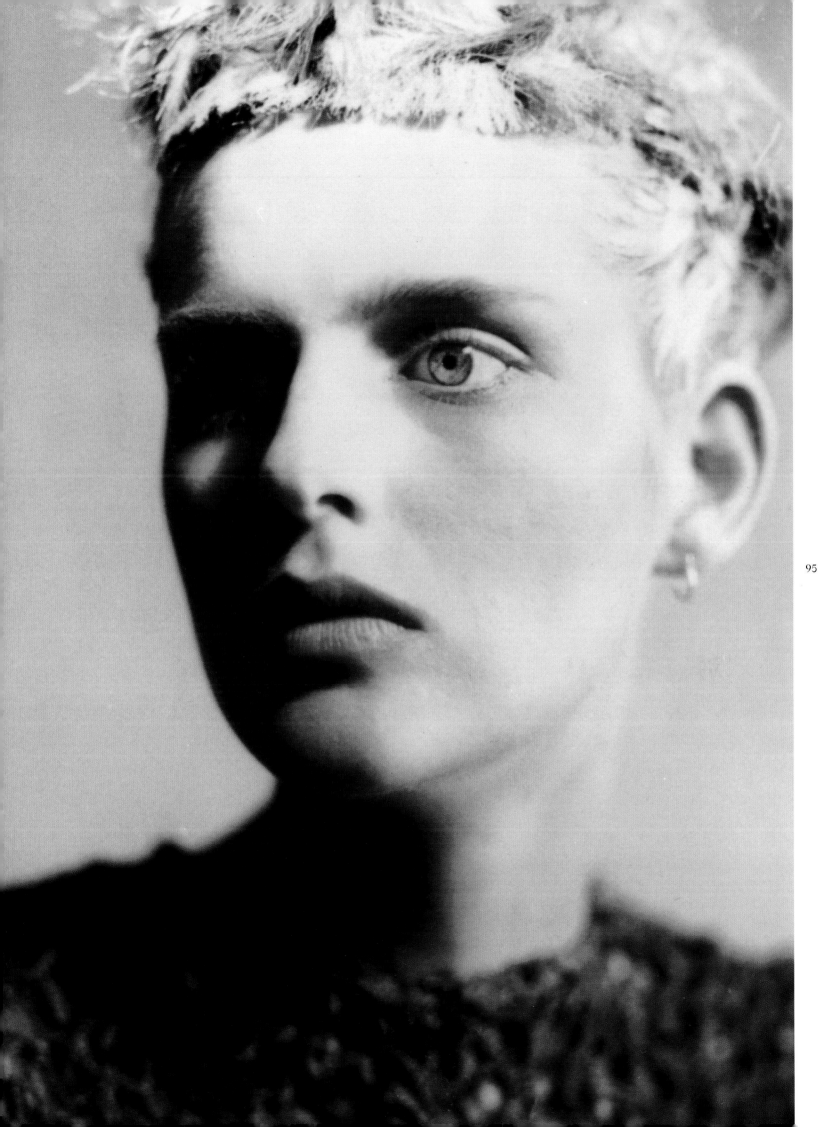

OPPOSITE · Personal picture of Bambi.
ABOVE · Autumn/Winter 1994–1995—photographer Juergen Teller.

97

98

ABOVE · *Bambi*, 2003, Edward Lipski.
OPPOSITE · Autumn/Winter 1993–1994—photographer Marc Hispard, model Kate Moss.

I who didn't really like expressing myself with words . . . always told Frédéric to speak about my collections with the runway shows' music . . . it was more personal, intimate, and especially stronger.

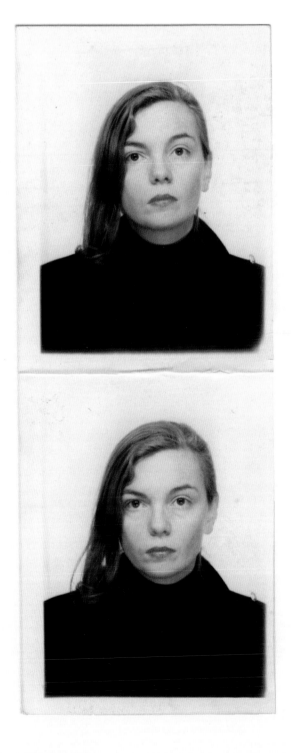

Polaroid and photo booth shots of Martine, 1992.

A PARALLEL UNIVERSE

Frédéric Sanchez

In the living room of a bourgeois apartment on the Rue Greffulhe, a little girl is sitting opposite a large whiteboard on which small sketches and pieces of fabric are lined up. A blue-eyed cat lies at her feet. It seems to be smiling.

She looks like Pearl in the Charles Laughton film, *The Night of the Hunter*.[1]

She rearranges some figurines one by one, putting them in order, then changing them around, while whispering stories to them that she has made up. It could be a scene from a Balthus painting, and the uncluttered room could be the decor in an Ibsen or Strindberg play. In front of an impressive chimney with lion's feet and an enormous mantelpiece decorated with an overlaid acanthus leaf pattern, two light-colored sofas sit facing each other. On the walls hang plates by Piero Fornassetti, all showing the same face, that of soprano Lina Cavalieri.

Everything is quiet. Only the ticking of a clock gives the impression of feeling time as it passes, of feeling every minute, and every instant.

The little girl gets up, moves away from the whiteboard and over to the window. She looks up at the sky and identifies a face in a cloud that seems to say to her: "Monkey gone to heaven."[2]

She turns around very quickly, for it seems to her that she can hear a strange noise coming from somewhere, and she discovers a blond woman who lives and sings "In Heaven" from the soundtrack of David Lynch's *Eraserhead* on a small music hall stage, hiding in one of the living room radiators:

Everything is terribly vague, and she loses her train of thought . . .

At the same time, a white rabbit dressed in a tuxedo comes in saying these words:

"spirit in the sky, spirit in the sky" . . . [3]

He finds a television and a video recorder, into which he slides a VHS cassette. The images are those of the dance scene (to the sound of "Kool Thing" by Sonic Youth [4] from Hal Hartley's film, *Simple Men*, a tribute to Jean-Luc Godard's film, *Bande à part.*

A certain tension can be felt owing to the dissonant sounds. We no longer know if we are hearing the ticking of the clock or the footsteps of the old retired colonel who lives in the apartment upstairs, furious about all this agitation. It is true that the world is much changed since Reynaldo Hahn: violence and passion.

Once again the little girl stands in front of the whiteboard, and her eyes sparkle, for they are permeated by the sounds; the images she has invented turn to dreams.

On the calm and black wave where stars sleep
The white Ophelia floats like a big lily,
Floating very slowly, asleep on her sails
—One hears in the faraway woods killings. [5]

Meanwhile, we seem to perceive a monotonous faraway song.
Seven pale, diaphanous figures appear deep inside the mirror over the fireplace. Like Bluebeard's wives, they seem to be dawn goddesses. One by one, they address the little girl.

Shalom:
"I came to your party dressed as a shadow." [6]

Kirsten:
At five o'clock under the clock, is it a stranger I will be looking for? [7]

Marie Sophie:
"*Mes regrets.*" [8]

Susie:
"Walk this way, walk this way." [9]

Stella:
"I'm sticking with you." [10]

Amber:
"Only Shallow." [11]

Lucie:
"Ladies and gentlemen I would like to introduce
to you the only gnome who wears habitually a 1912 bathing costume." [12]

They disappear in a flash of light.

Enter Mimi, wearing a dress of raw silk, her blond hair contained under an immense wide-brimmed hat. Kate and a Japanese madman shout: "*Shingayo*!!!! *Shingayo*!!!!" [13] They take the little girl by the hand and walk her through the mirror.

Just then, the living room turns dark, the walls grow to make place for an immense room that was once a theater at the foot of a hill in Montmartre. And in this Expressionist decor, the electric sounds *Akathisia* of the group Hovercraft [14] are heard alongside the synthetic sounds of Add N to (X). [15]

Suddenly a telephone rings and a voice says:
"May I speak to Martine?"

1 — Pearl's song, "Once Upon a Time There Was a Pretty Fly" in the film *The Night of the Hunter* by Charles Laughton.

2 — "Monkey Gone to Heaven" is a track from the 1989 Pixies album *Doolittle*.

3 — "Spirit in the Sky" is a 1986 cover version, by Doctor and The Medics, of a song written and performed by Norman Greenbaum in 1969.

4 — "Kool Thing" is a track from the 1990 Sonic Youth album *Goo*.

5 — Arthur Rimbaud's "Ophélie."

6 — "I Came to Your Party Dressed as a Shadow" is a 2001 track by the group Piano Magic.

7 — "Waiting" is a Hermine Demoriane song from her 1982 record *The World Is On My Plates*. Lyrics by Ian Kane.

8 — *"Mes regrets"* is a Michel Polnareff song from 1967.

9 — "Walk This Way" is an Aerosmith track. In 1986 a new version was recorded with the rap group Run-D.M.C.

10 — "I'm Sticking With You" is a track by The Velvet Underground from *VU*, the album of previously unreleased tracks that came out in 1985.

11 — "Only Shallow" is a track from the 1991 My Bloody Valentine album, *Loveless*.

12 — "Radio Gnome Invisible" is a track from the 1977 Gong album, *Gong Live!*

13 — *Excrete Music* is a 1991 album by the group Violent Onsen Geisha.

14 — *Akathisia* is a 1996 album by the experimental rock group Hovercraft.

15 — *Avant Hard* is a 1999 album by the group Add N to (X).

107

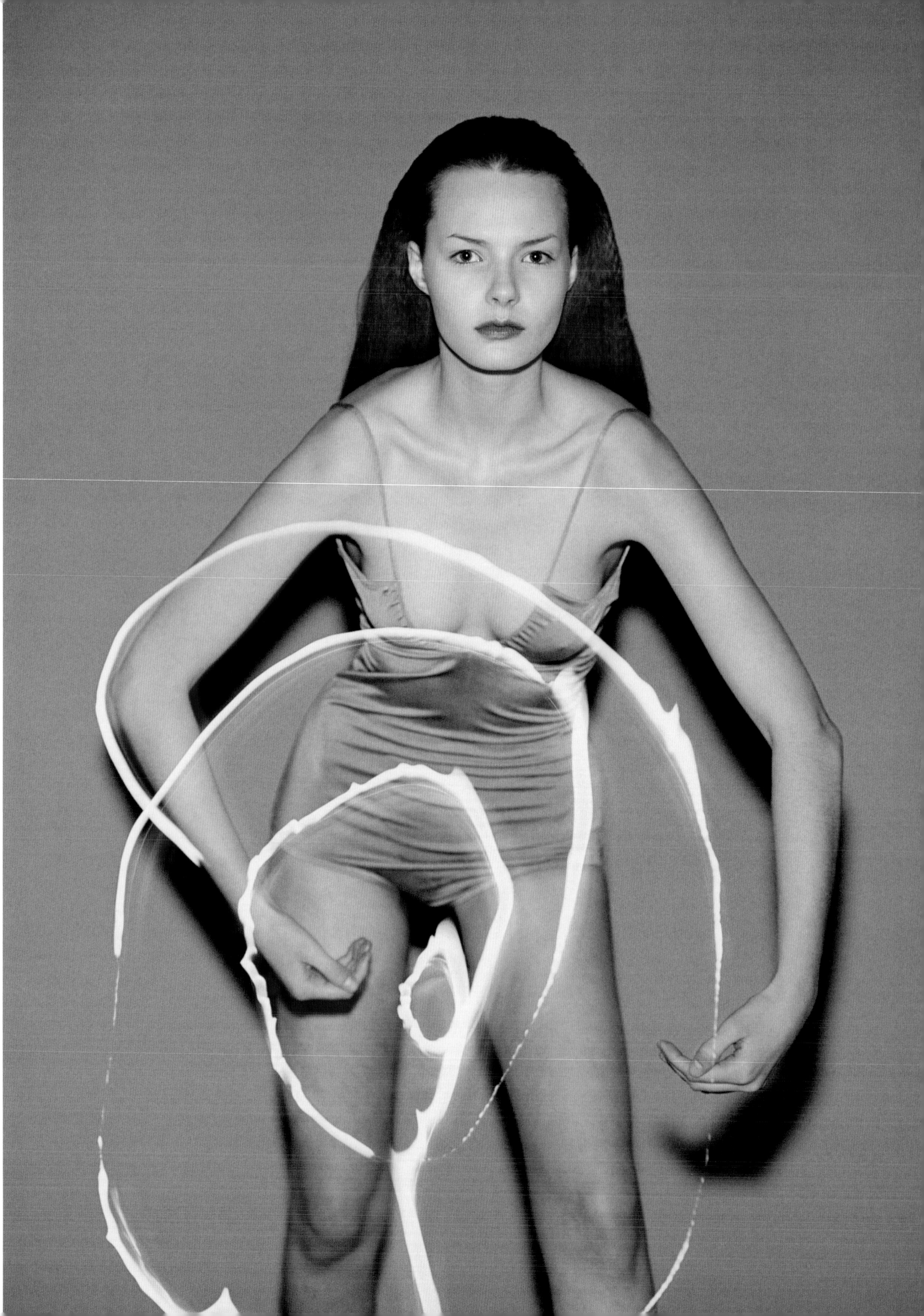

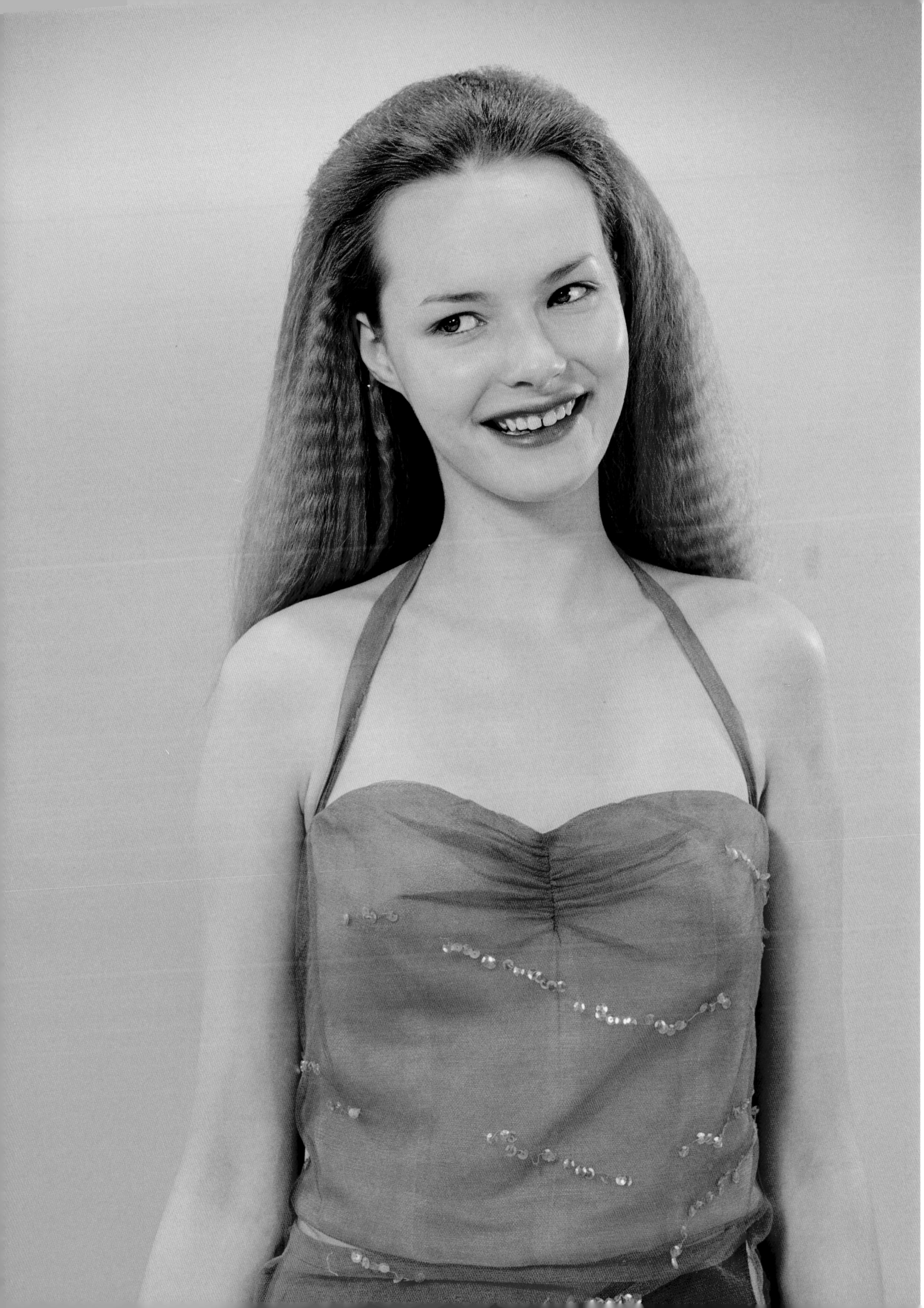

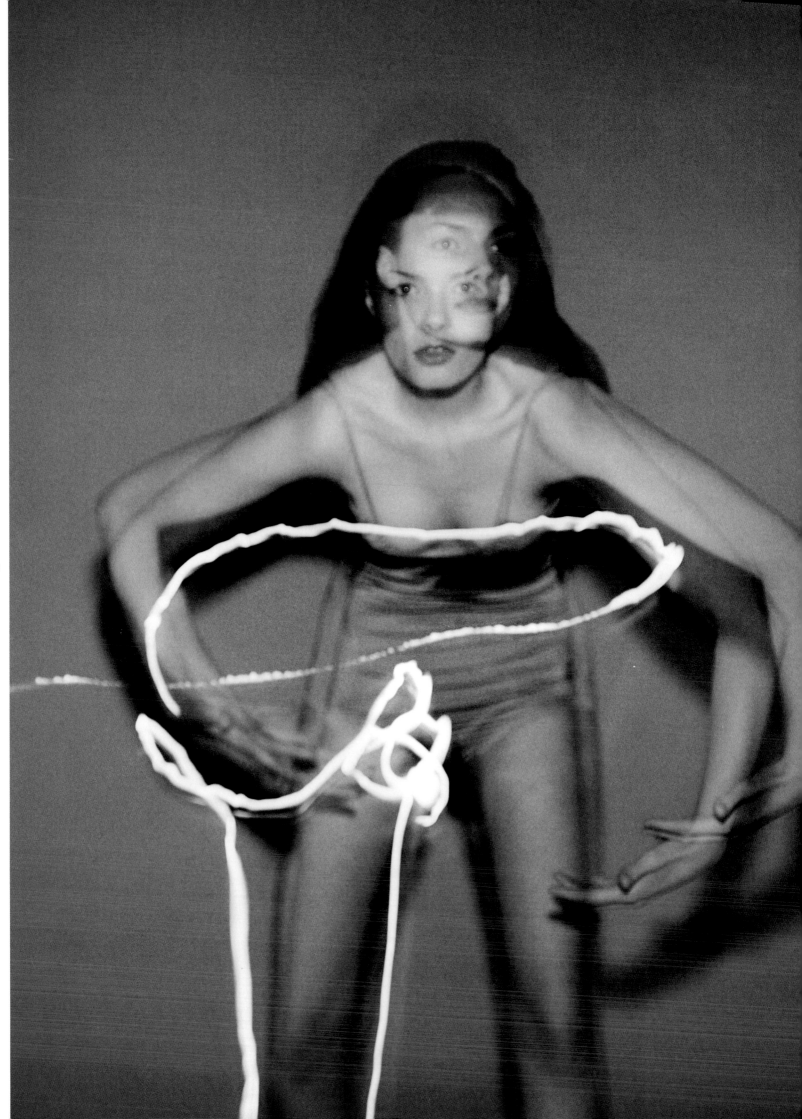

118

120

Research photos for my collection based on dance.

Guinevere Van Seenus backstage at the Spring/Summer 1997 runway show.

128

Kate in Linda Cantello's magical makeup.

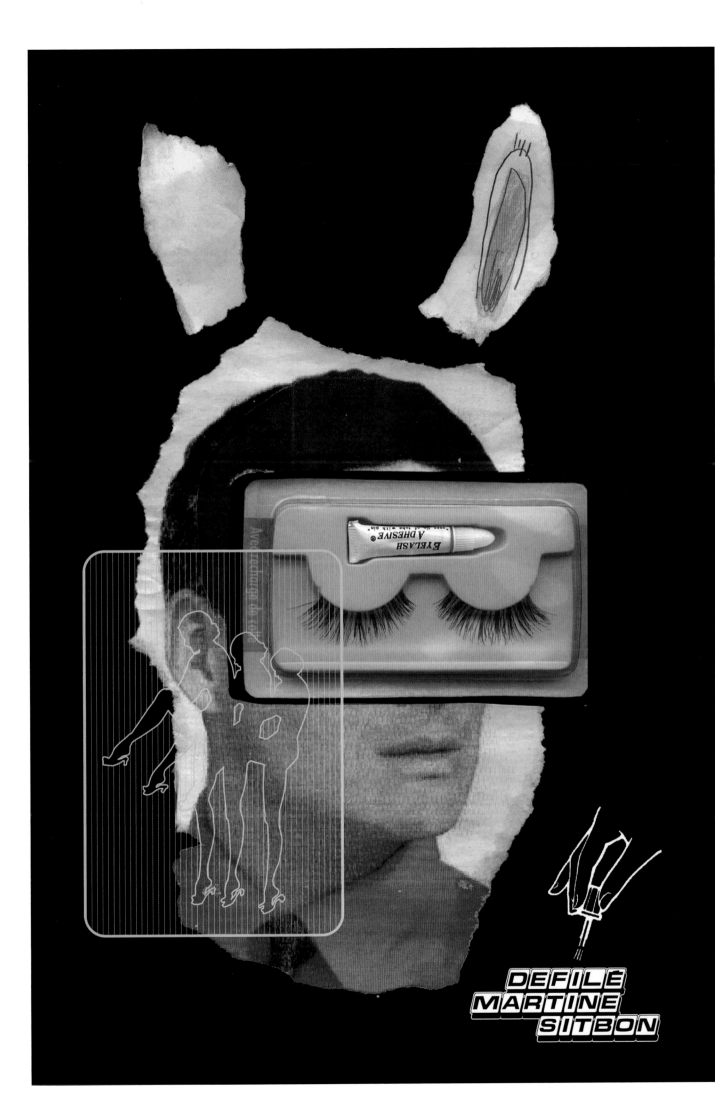

Spring/Summer 1997—photographer Horst Diekgerdes, model Devon Aoki.

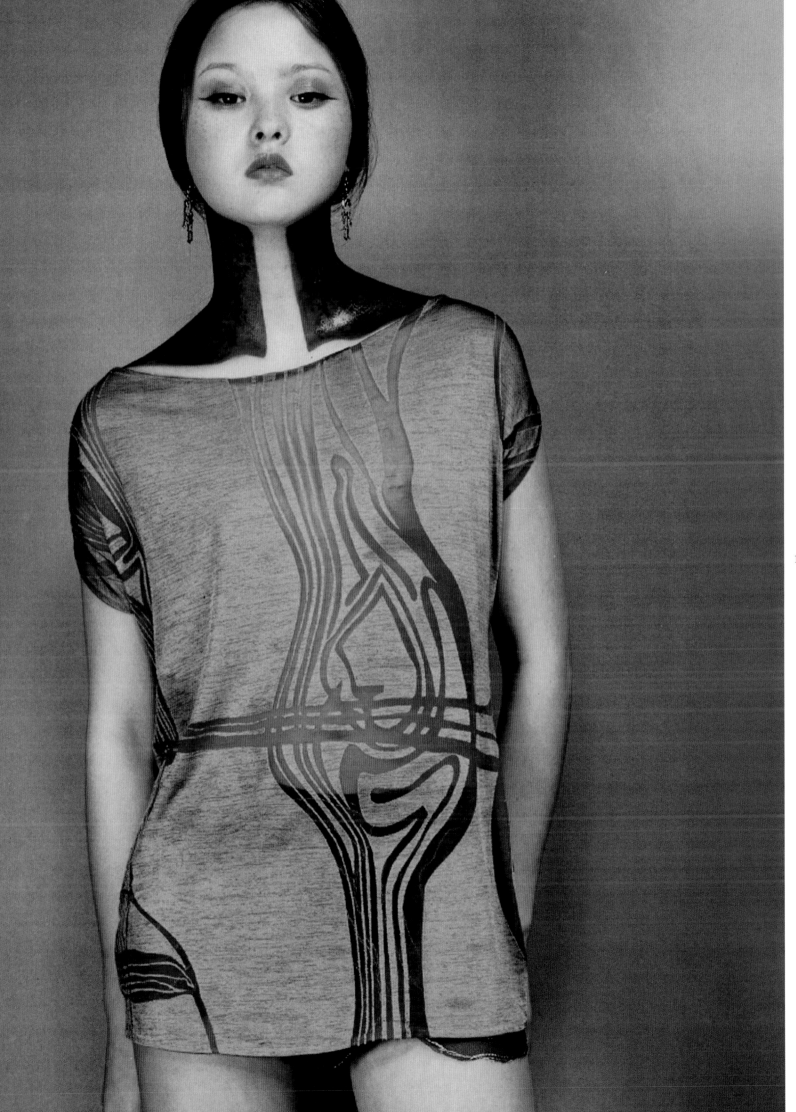

ABOVE · Top with application on silk tulle, Autumn/Winter 1997–1998 collection.
OPPOSITE · Autumn/Winter 1997–1998—photograph in *i-D* magazine.
FOLLOWING PAGES · Silk georgette dress, Autumn/Winter 1997–1998 collection.

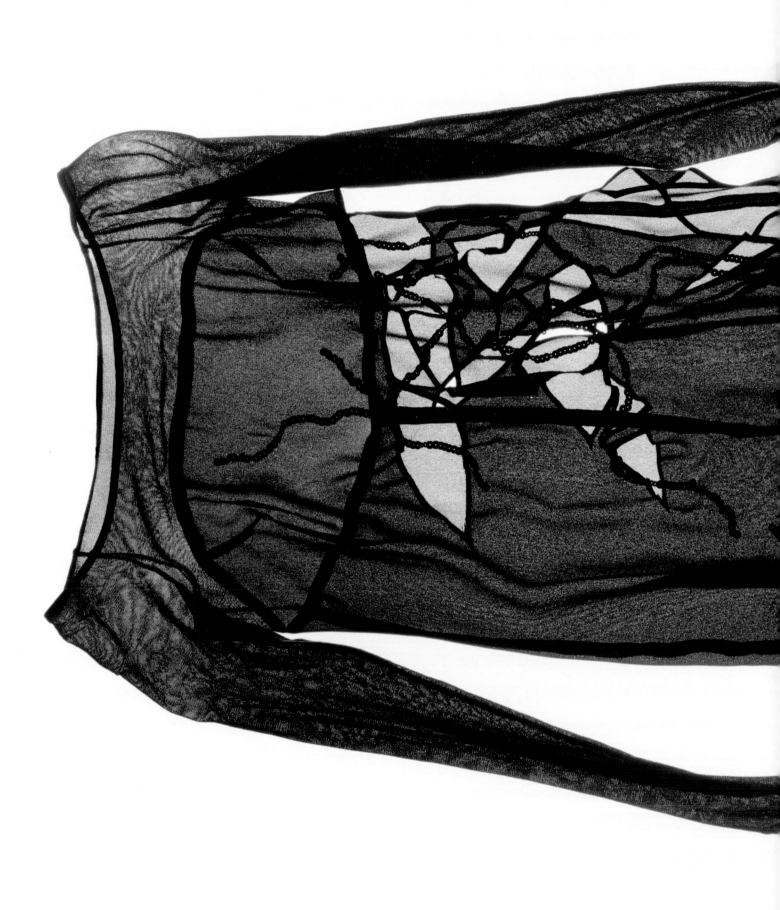

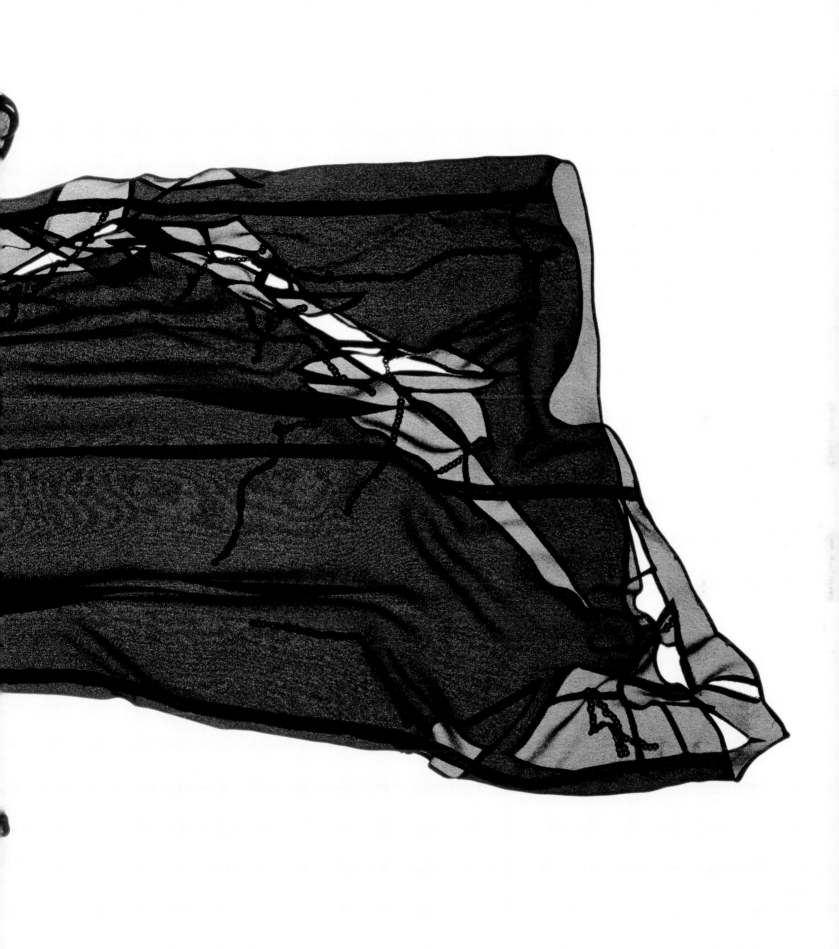

ABOVE, OPPOSITE, AND FOLLOWING PAGES · Autumn/Winter 1997–1998 catalog—photographer Craig McDean, model Stella Tennant.

Personal notebook, Autumn/Winter 1997–1998 collection "*Les Arbres*," Camille Bidault-Waddington fitting Polaroids.

142

A delicate illustration by Anita Pallenberg that I really love.

OPPOSITE · Autumn/Winter 1997–1998—photograph in *W* magazine, model Missy Rayder.
FOLLOWING PAGES · Personal notebook, Autumn/Winter 1997–1998 collection "*Les Arbres*," Camille Bidault-Waddington
and Susanne D. fitting Polaroids

F16

148

DEFILE Martine Sitbon DEFILE

PREVIOUS PAGES · Autumn/Winter 1997-1998—photographer Jean-Baptiste Mondino, model Alek Wek (French *Vogue*).
ABOVE · Invitation to the Spring/Summer 1997 runway show, concept and illustration M/M Paris.
OPPOSITE AND PAGE 151 · Autumn/Winter 1997-1998—photographer Satoshi Saïkusa, model Danielle Zinaich (*Frank* magazine).

Portrait of Martine by Jean-Baptiste Mondino.

INDEPENDENCE DAYS

Fabrice Paineau

Everything must have begun in 1994, when I was a student and she was
a designer. She turned up alone in the classroom to explain cinema
and fashion in her own terms, timidly at first, then more confidently
towards the end of the session. She wore her dark glasses—the stamp
of Parisian creatures for whom the day never ends and who launch
a certain type of debate. She was hard at work at the time. Her recent
show, for Spring/Summer 1995, had attracted quite a lot of attention.
It was aimed, first of all, at those who had a certain eye for fashion,
then at those for whom it was only just attainable—these new young
women whom she planned to dress. It had everything in it: photography
from an era that was moving towards cockney realism; images
by David Sims and Corinne Day; and the jubilatory and grunge *laisser-
aller* of independent magazines. In addition, there was her way
of treating clothes that was so unique with this high-end and low-end
style that she sort of invented at that moment in time—either on
her own or with the help of her partner, artistic director Marc Ascoli.
She, for example, gave us peroxide hair made dirty for the occasion and
different faces—girls who looked like they'd been out all night at
the Marquee Club, or who were straight out of a Mick Rock book.
They were good days.

And then, of course, there were the clothes. They acknowledged a very modern balance that was both serene and wild, with flea market finds repaired by seamstresses in the ateliers—her own ateliers, for she intended to keep the "house" aspect of handmade craftsmanship and the precise science of the editorial.

"Since 1986 I'd been having fun, and yes, I gave Kristen McMenamy dragonfly wings and put three hats on Susie Bick, but then, I wanted to dress the girls, the ones that I couldn't see in the streets yet. I was already thinking of giving them parkas to wear over evening dresses so that they could go out freely." At that point in time, it was called "doing what you wanted." A few years later, it was called styling. Or what to wear with what. And then adding a dissolute touch to the look to create the charm of strange beauty. Nothing too accessible, though.

This formula was later widely industrialized by consultants and advisors, and in commentaries by major brands. The latter employed photo stylists in order to add a touch of this untidiness to their well-oiled machine.

Martine's dream was to give form to that which she wanted to present. She preferred allure over silhouette. She liked faces, personalities, and strong girls with character, even if some of them looked like angels. Like Kirsten Owen, who she discovered by chance in the corridors of the Pin-up photo studio as she was getting ready to shoot her collection with photographer Javier Vallhonrat, under the watchful eye of Marc Ascoli. "She looked like those diaphanous girls from the '70s. We couldn't believe it! We took her on right away. It was her first photo shoot." The images of these diaphanous girls or others from the '60s, '70s, and '80s weren't things that she had taken from the photo archives that are useful to know about. They had been stuck on her bedroom walls. There is an Alain Bashung song that comes to mind now, where he mentions how he created the season in his cranium. For her, the season was to be a long one, and it began in that bedroom. Or perhaps it began as she went to buy bread, going down the road and coming face-to-face with James Dean on the original poster for *Rebel Without a Cause,* where he's holding a knife. "I fell in love with him. I went back indoors to see my sisters and proclaim my love for this guy in the white T-shirt." They laughed at her. "They told me that he had been dead for a long time. I felt stupid. But it was perhaps my first love affair with film." From then on, when she wasn't hiding under her bed sheets listening to Radio Luxembourg on her transistor radio, she was watching films. Dreyer's *The Passion of Joan of Arc,* Charles Laughton's *The Night of the Hunter,* Jacques Tourneur's films, and so on. The girl was a walking film library. This was precocious for fourteen. Then she started going out, ran away a bit thanks to her friends. She even went on a school trip to Brighton and London so that she could go to concerts and go out to nightclubs. All of that suited her better. The music in these clubs resembled what she listened to on her transistor at night.

There was always this music of her own. It took up space in her brain and she fixated on different eras, for her centers of interest were extremely varied. Here is a non-exhaustive list of the greatest: Marc Bolan, David Bowie, The Velvet Underground, and the charming Edie Sedgwick, among others. "I had no problem idealizing them as I knew only the best—the words, the music, and only the good side of these adults from a sometimes superior generation."

This passion led her much later to fashion, taking her by surprise as she transformed all these costumes of the heroes she listened to into suitable clothes. Taking her sister's advice—the one who had laughed at her for being in love with James Dean—she happened to get into the Studio Berçot fashion design school, run by Marie Rucki. "If I hadn't met someone open-minded like Marie, I wouldn't have stayed in fashion." It was now time for that cranium to open up.

So, let me come back to 1995, nine years after she started out in 1986. I arrived the following year at the Rue Braque, where she had her studio and her home. These two floors were a hive of activity with people everywhere. In the second-floor atelier there weren't many French people; it was filled with occasionally shambolic savants who arrived from English schools such as Central Saint Martins, or from more exotic locations such as Iceland. She was one of the first to welcome them, and the formula would be taken up by others. And all of that formed a sort of school where each person endeavored to show their teeming creativity. Influences were diverse. The high and low style described earlier was in full swing. A finely worked, embroidered, and deformed sweatshirt was slipped on under a mousseline dress with *dévoré* velvet panels like an angular Mackintosh pattern. Dyeing was done right in the big sinks near the kitchen in exhilarating DIY style. The Parisian underground had found its very own playground right here.

The first hours in the creative process of a collection are always somewhat abstract. Martine Sitbon let her rainbow-haired recruit, Julie Verhoeven, begin with a drawing. "I used to draw, but then I left it to these guys, who, with a few strokes, could sketch the indisputable lines of our conversations. Then I would take over as designer. We would transform it as we went." She let the girls in. Some were famous, such as Kate Moss on French soil for the first time, who Martine had already noticed in her first editorial on the cover of *The Face,* shot by Corinne Day. She says "Kate was so sweet and incredibly fresh with her biker boots, little legs, and bad-boy style." Others were less well-known, such as Hélène Blais, who designed her shoes, or Camille Bidault-Waddington, one of her muses, ready to try on anything and who learned fashion design from the catwalks. She surrounded herself with these inspiring women, without knowing that her little Factory was filled with promise for them too. The press considered her to be the little English woman on the continent; Martine herself thought that she had created a real gang of girls. They embodied Paris and didn't intend leaving the city in the near future. "I began to love Paris when I had catwalk shows. There were all these faces and I wanted to give them clothes so that they would get on well in this city." But she let the wind blow between the streets. Helmut Lang held a show in Paris, but was already dreaming of Donald Judd and the great New York galleries. Jean Colonna had taken up in just one area, the east of Paris—that was enough. Certain Americans were afraid to go there. Martine was looking for an underground Paris capable of creating links with London and New York. "And what was I supposed to do? I was Parisian." Martine was already knowledgeable about editorials, which defined the capital with spot-on precision. Of course she created strong clothes—*dévoré* pieces and appliqué work like those trees that were straight out of a Tim Burton forest. But she could also impose nothing more than a lilac leather skirt paired with a slightly intricate top. This equilibrium began to prosper everywhere just when the runway was becoming a regulator for thought processes. It was another way to establish the intention of balancing a demonstration of strength with a commercial foundation.

At the end of the 1990s, in this game of fashion propositions, casting, and fashion design—all overlaid with a layer of fine culture—Martine Sitbon wrote the formulas that would establish a new world. Expertise entered the catwalk environs, except that Martine designed above all for girls who liked surprises. She offered them a giant, adjustable mood board. Many others would benefit from this. And as for Martine, well . . . she kept her dark glasses on.

158

162

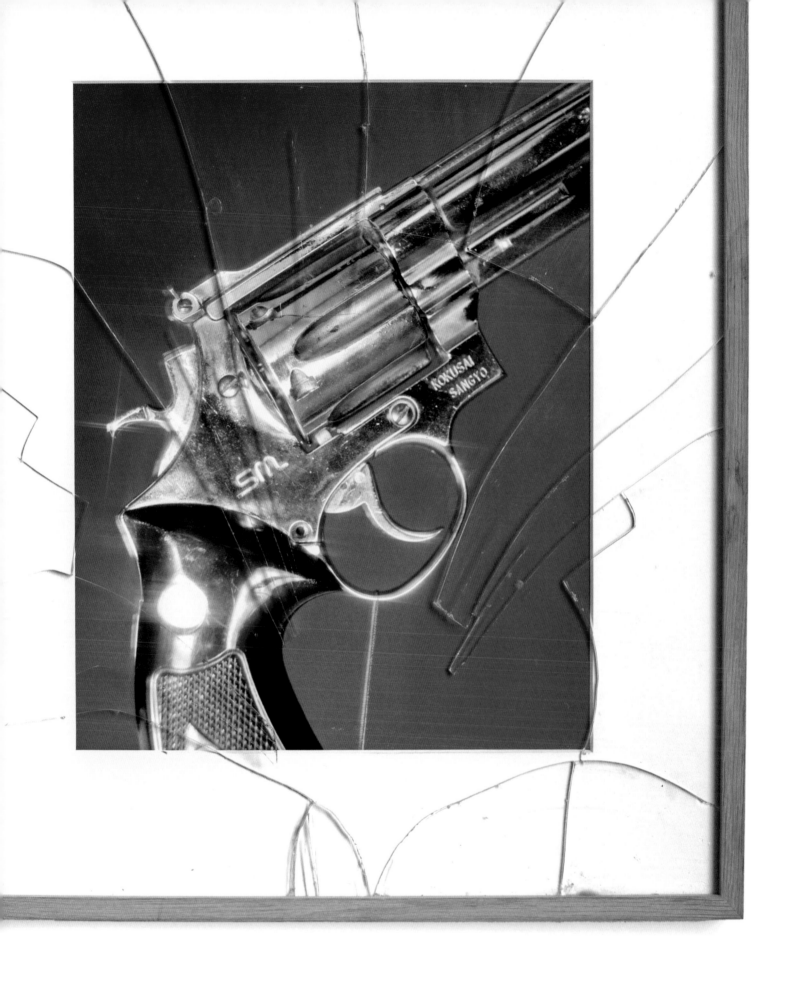

ABOVE · Cracked frame, personal archives—photographer Craig McDean.
OPPOSITE · Autumn/Winter 1997–1998—photographer Craig McDean, model Camille Bidault-Waddington, graphic design M/M Paris.

A photo for my sunglasses license in Japan.

166

AUTOMNE-HIVER 1994/95 • Lundi 7 Mars 1994 à 18h30 • École des Beaux-Arts – 14, rue Bonaparte, Paris VI • P.R. Michèle Montagne (1) 42 03 81 00 • Showroom 6, rue de Braque Paris III (1) 48 87 37 47

OPPOSITE · Invitation to the Autumn/Winter 1994–1995 runway show, concept and illustration M/M Paris.
ABOVE · Invitation to the Autumn/Winter 1996–1997 runway show, concept and illustration M/M Paris.
FOLLOWING PAGES · Invitation to the Autumn/Winter 1999–2000 runway show, concept and illustration M/M Paris.

168

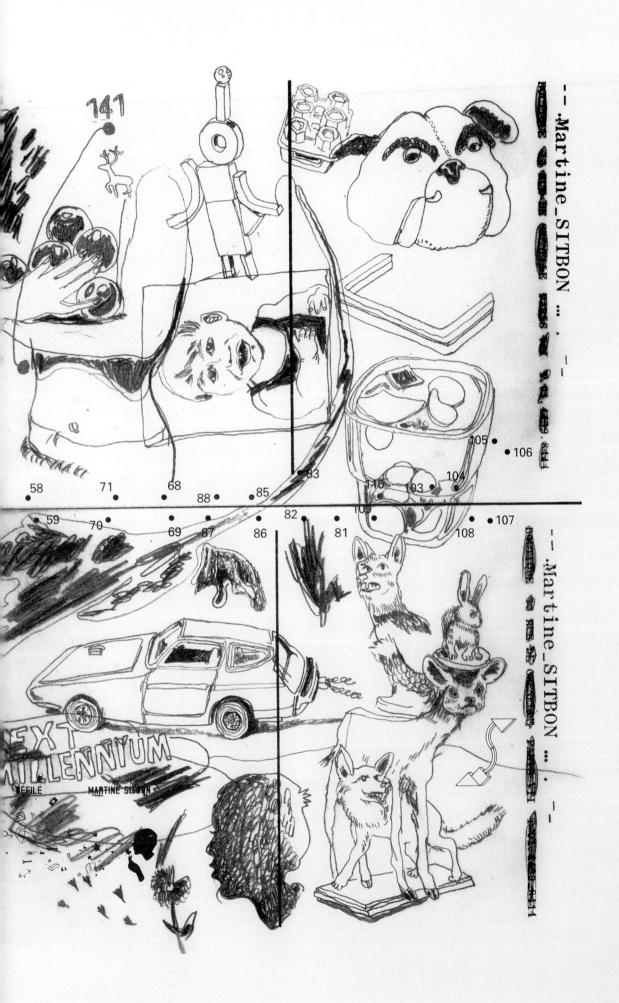

Personal notebook, Spring/Summer 1998 collection *"Aplats de Couleur,"* inspirations, Polaroids, fittings, color swatches, and fabric samples.

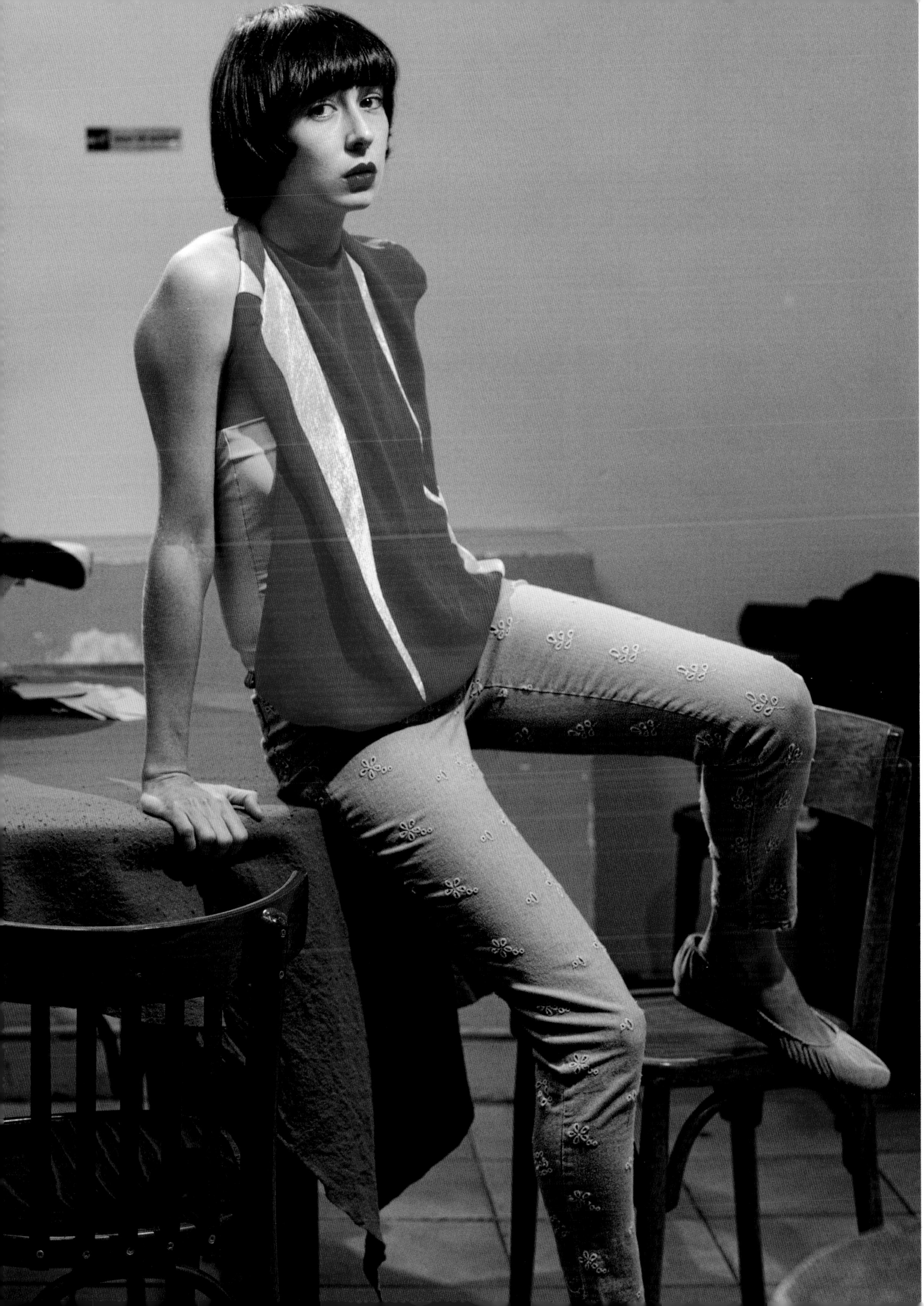

174

PREVIOUS PAGES · Spring/Summer 1998—photographer Alexei Hay, model Camille Bidault-Waddington (*Self Service* magazine).
ABOVE · Spring/Summer 1998 casting Polaroid.
OPPOSITE · Velvet *dévoré* dress, Spring/Summer 1998 collection.
FOLLOWING PAGES
(176-177) · Spring/Summer 2000—photographer Peter Lindbergh, model Amber Valletta.
(178) · Personal notebook, Autumn/Winter 1998-1999 collection "Silver Eye/Rothko," pattern position placement/felt pattern
applied on silk mousseline and Polaroids for Linda Cantello's makeup.
(179) · Dress from the Autumn/Winter 1998-1999 collection—photographer Federico Berardi.
(180) · Dress from the Autumn/Winter 1998-1999 collection—photographer Federico Berardi.
(181) · Autumn/Winter 1998-1999 fitting Polaroid.

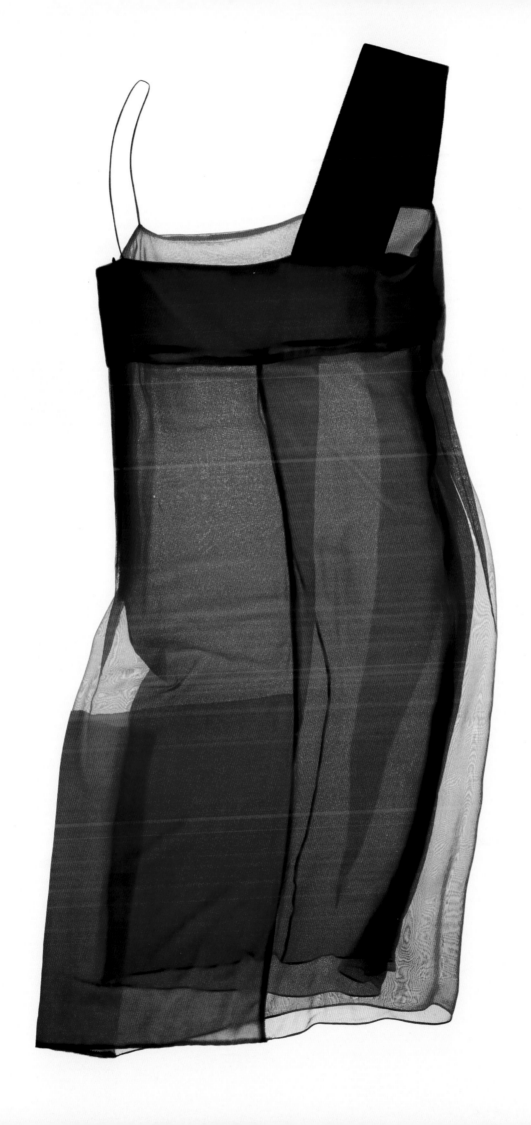

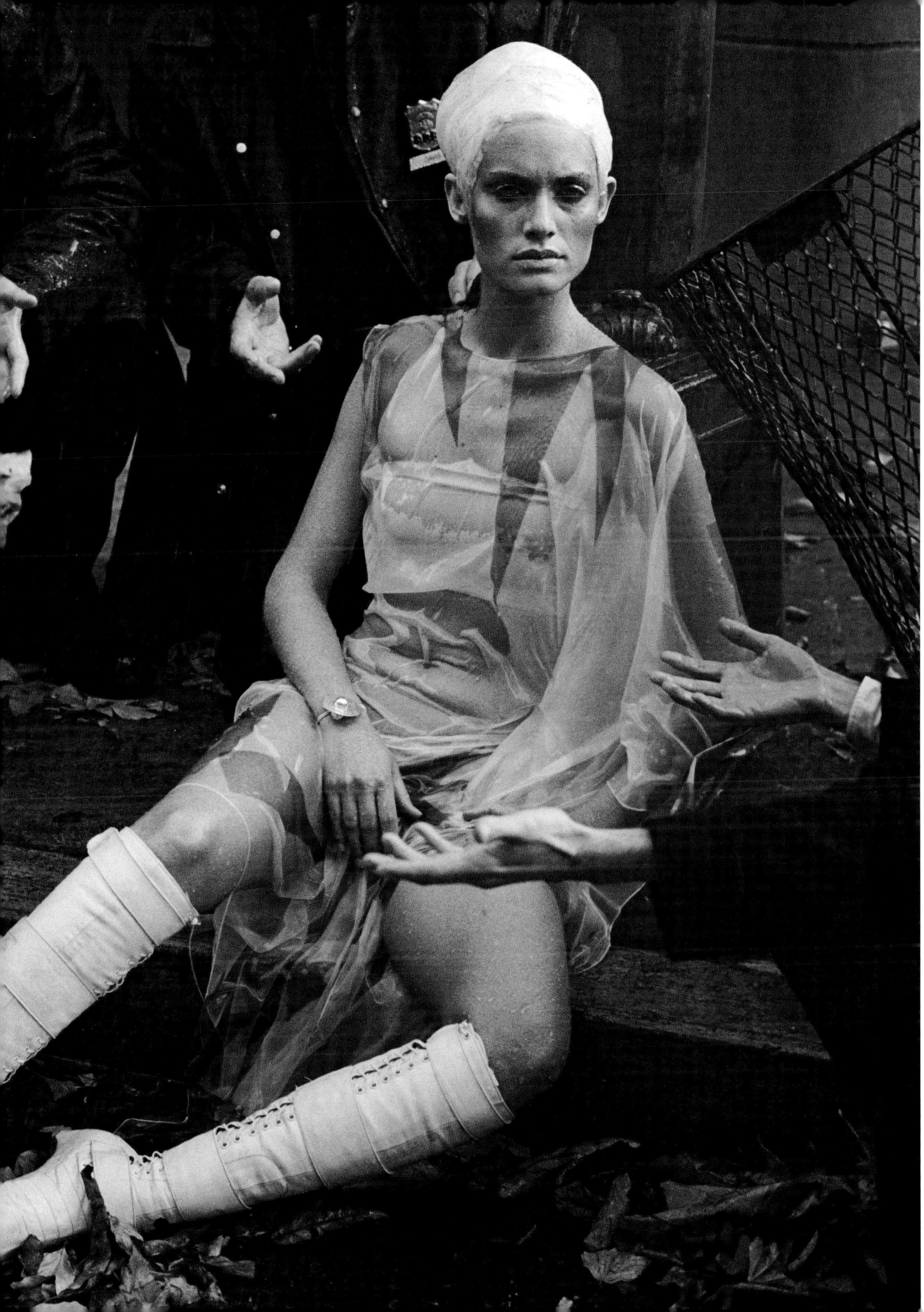

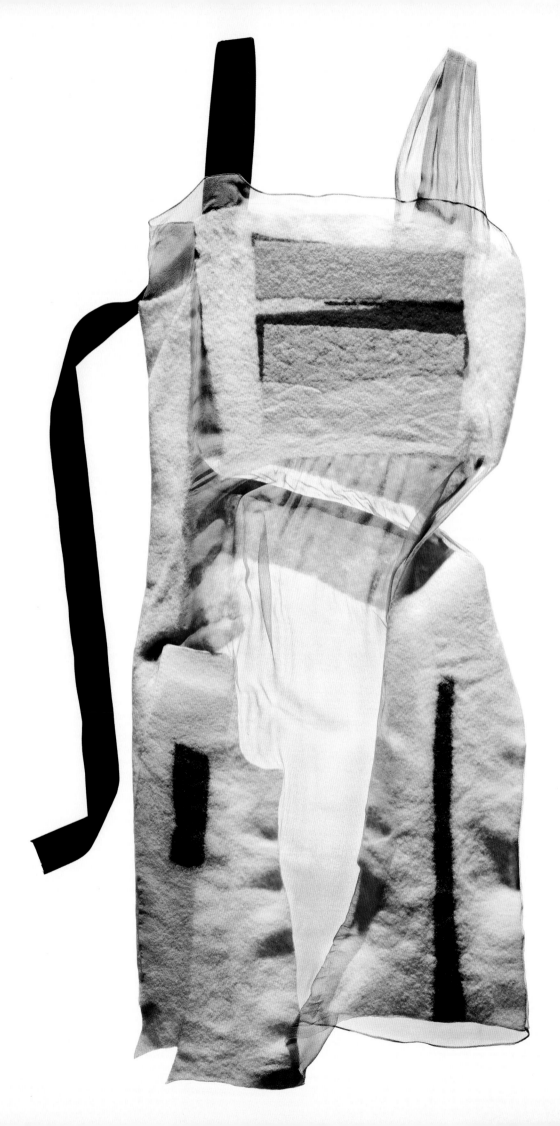

181

Detail of hand-carded vinyl resin material.

OPPOSITE · Spring/Summer 1999—photographer Jean-Baptiste Mondino, model Eva Herzigova.

FOLLOWING PAGES · Personal notebook, Spring/Summer 1999 collection "*Graphisme/Pois et Rayures*," images of inspirations and swatches for printed fabric.

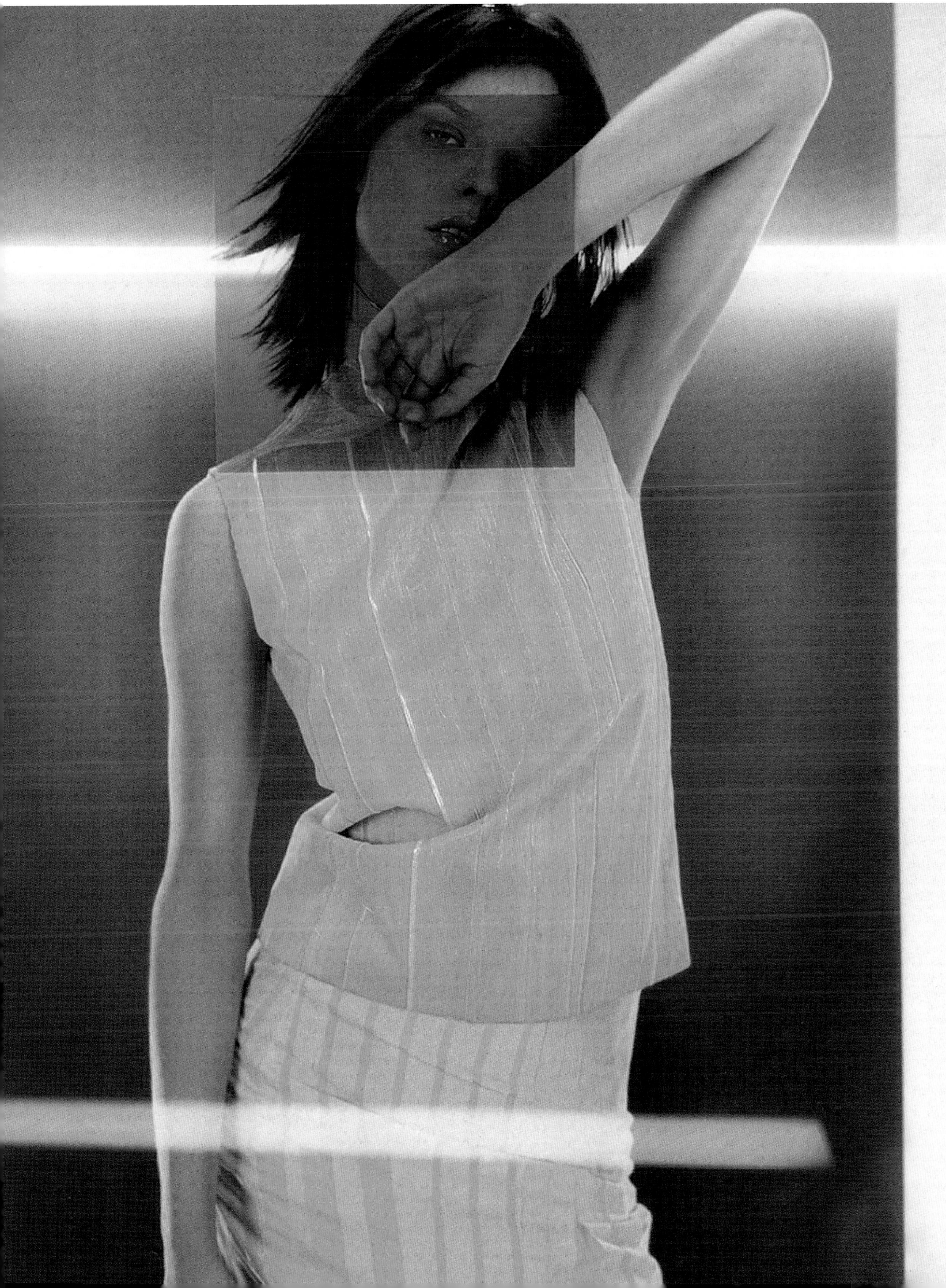

plession
wore open at back

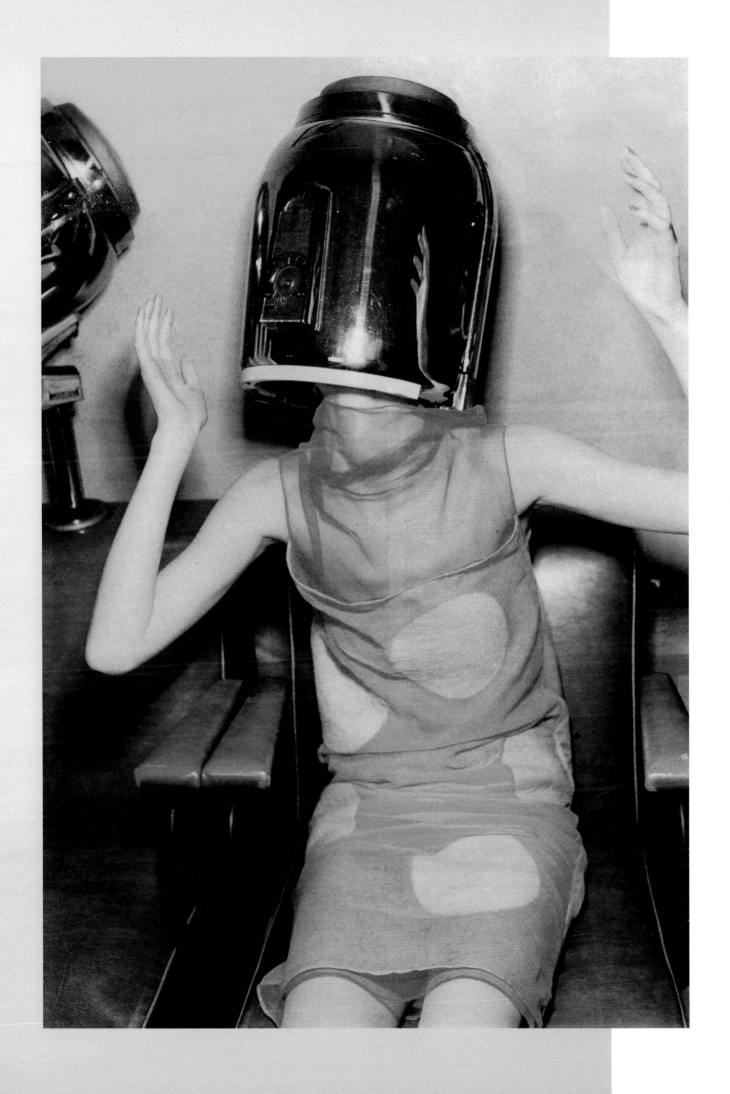

PREVIOUS PAGES
(186) · Sketches for the Spring/Summer 1999 collection.
(187) · Spring/Summer 1999—photographer Ellen von Unwerth (*Sud-Deutsche Zeitung*).
OPPOSITE · Spring/Summer 1999—photographer Mario Sorrenti, model Malgosia Bela (Italian *Vogue*).

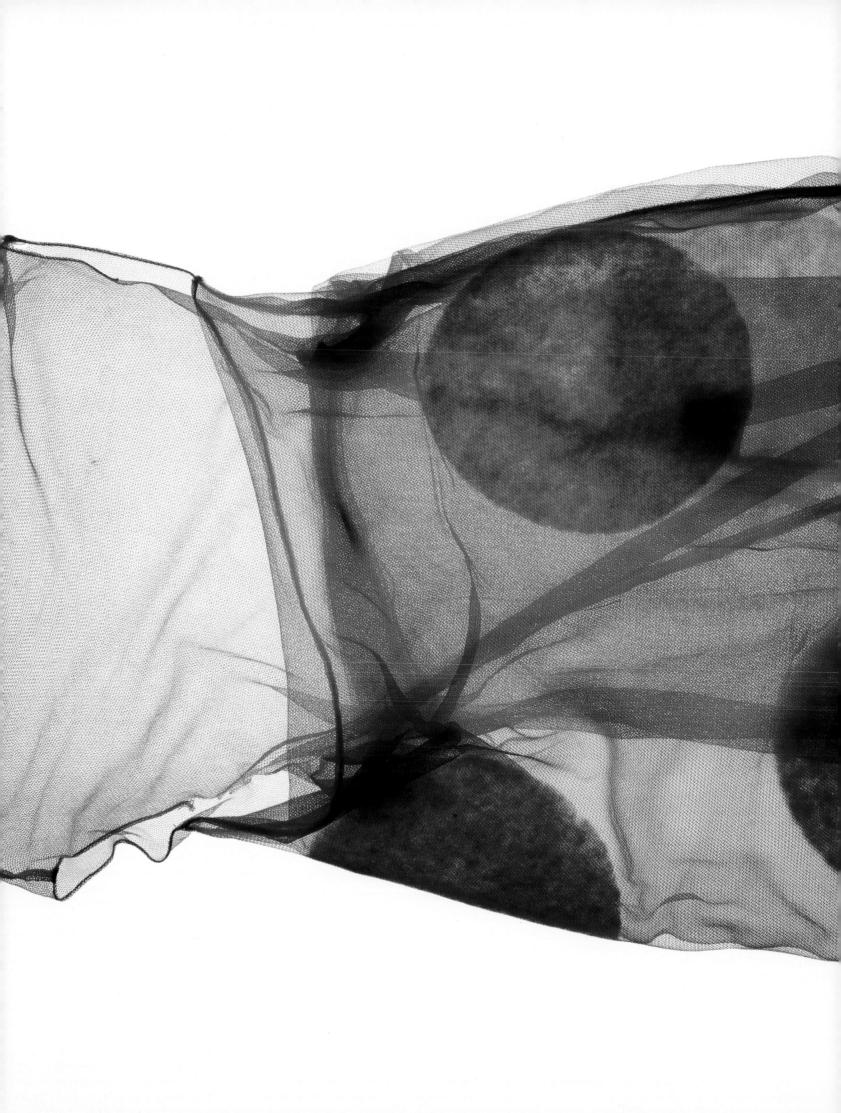

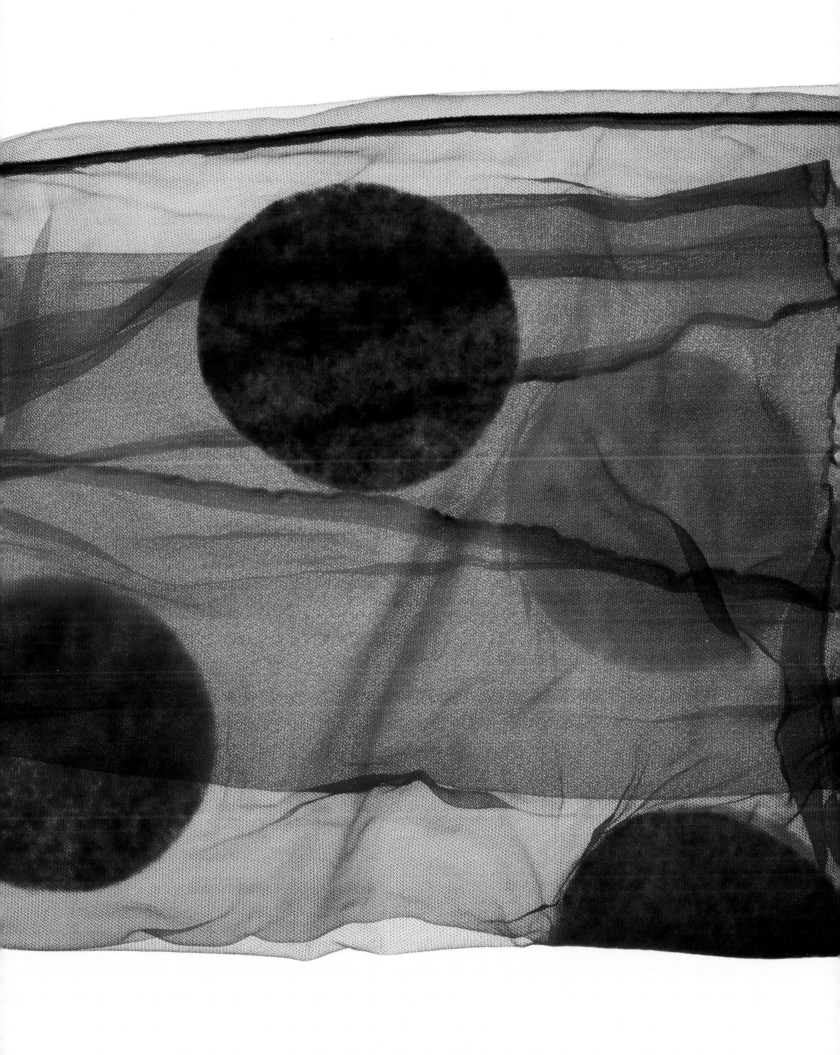

PREVIOUS PAGES · Dress from the Spring/Summer 1999 collection—photographer Federico Berardi.
OPPOSITE · Autumn/Winter 1999-2000—photographer Andrés Serrano, model Kirsten Owen (*Mixte*).
FOLLOWING PAGES · Drawings from the sales book for the Autumn/Winter 1999-2000 collection.

703

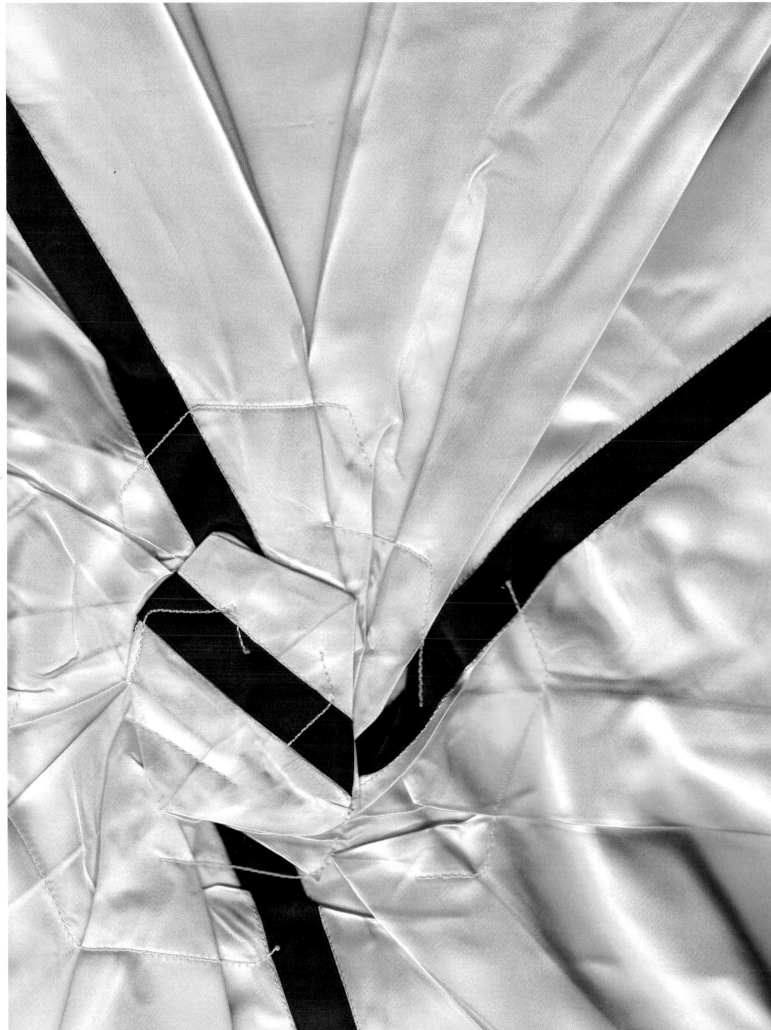

198

199

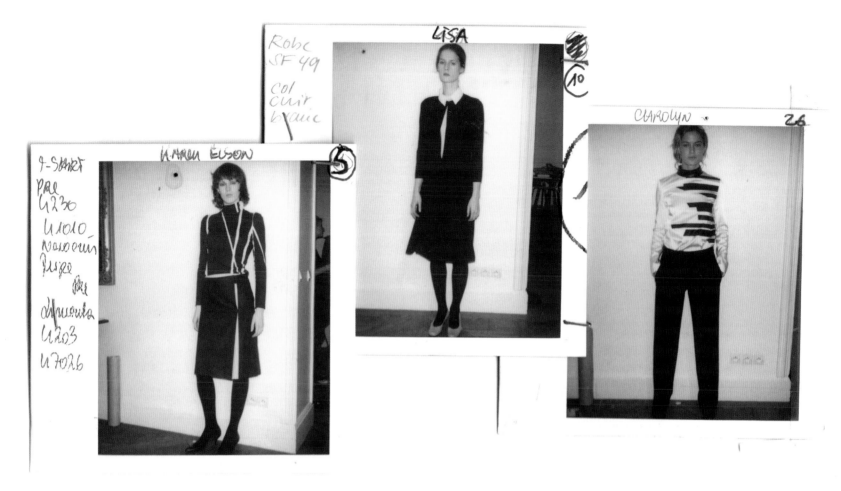

Model fittings for the Autumn/Winter 1999–2000 collection "Edward Scissorhands."

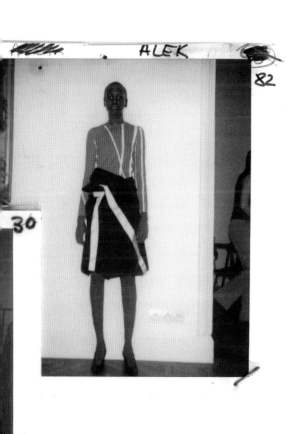

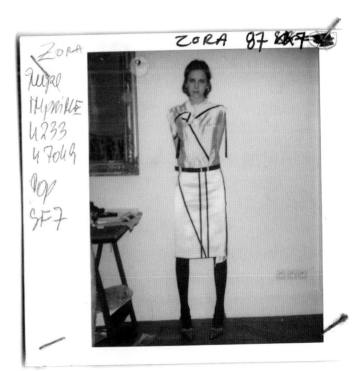

202

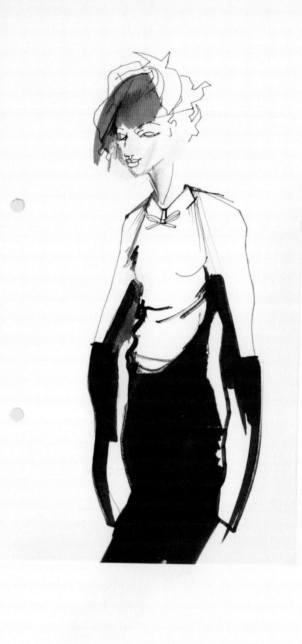

mixed embroide
chenile +

embroidered
accessory

OPPOSITE · Sketches from the Autumn/Winter 1999–2000 collection.
ABOVE · Casting Polaroid of Kirsten Owen.
FOLLOWING PAGES · Autumn/Winter 2001–2002—photographer Pierre Bailly (*The Face*).

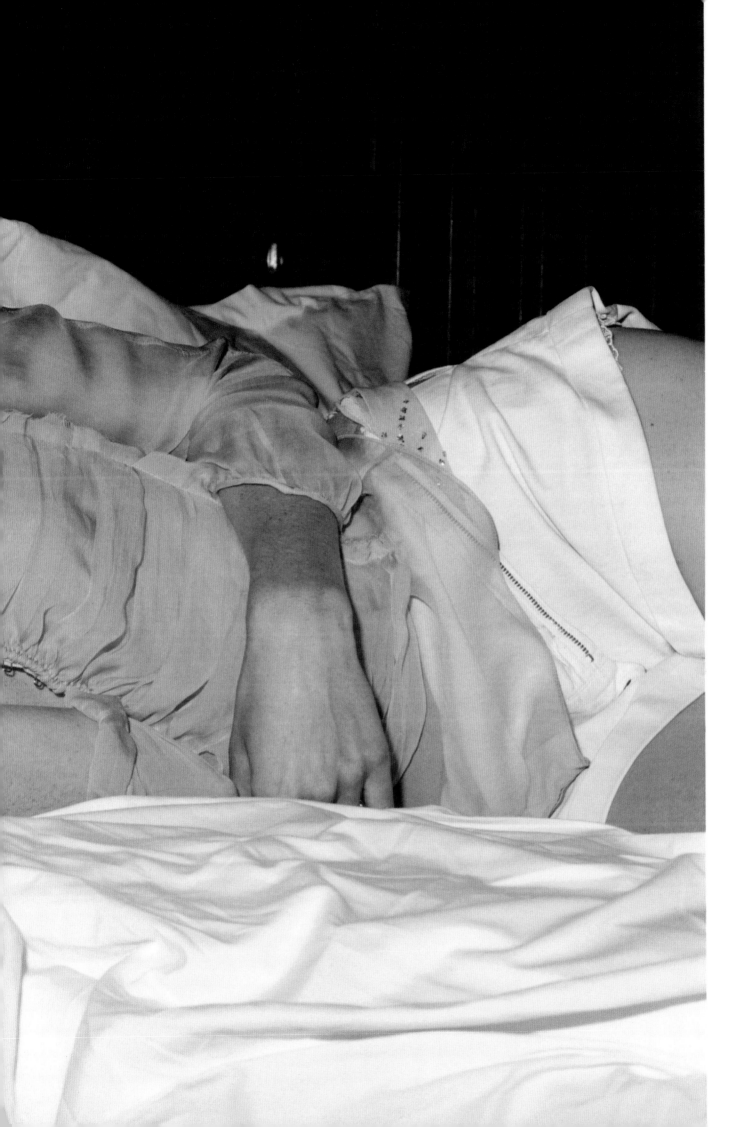

208

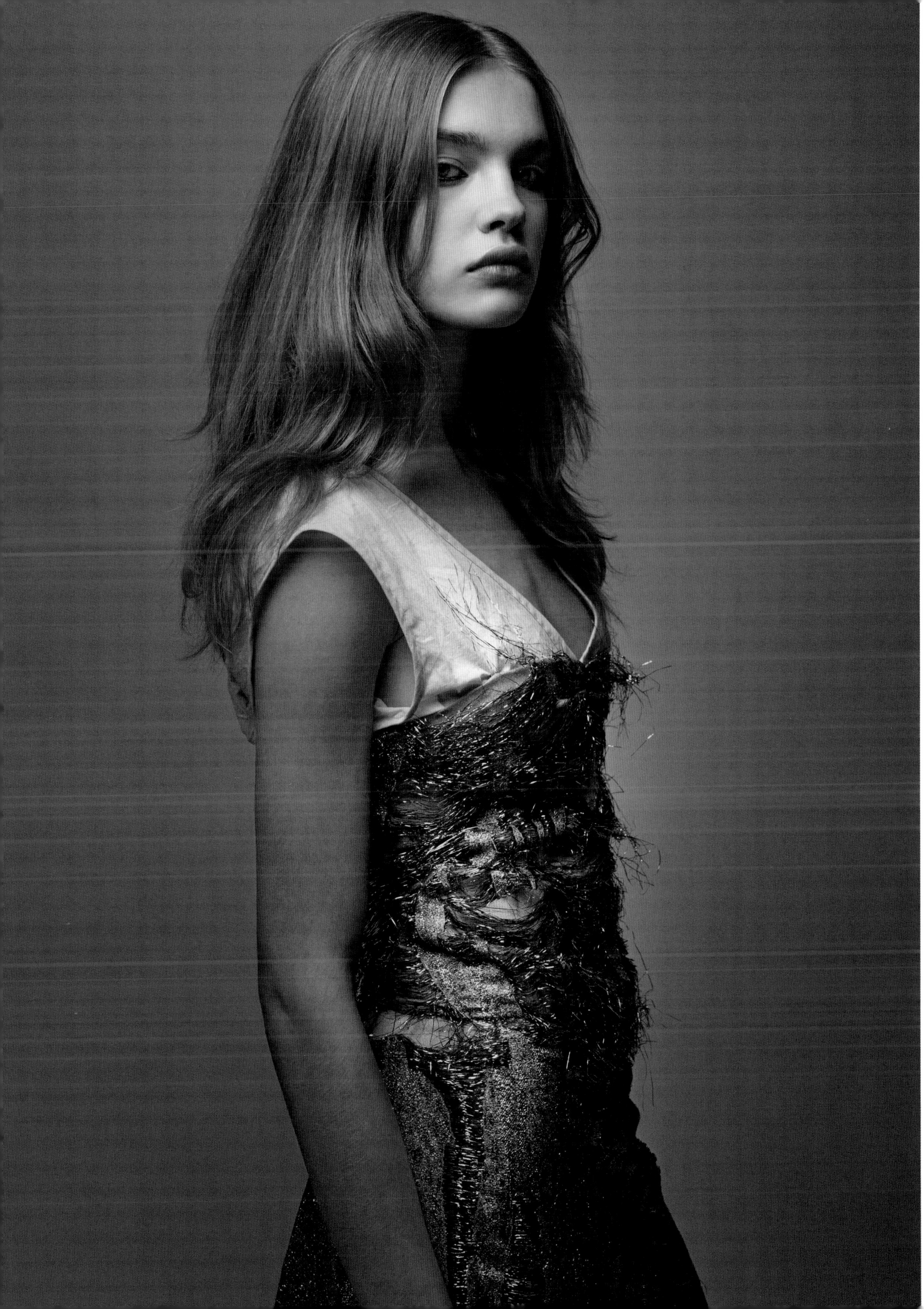

213

PREVIOUS PAGES
(208) · Autumn/Winter 2001-2002—photographer David Lasnet, model Stella Tennant (*Jalouse*).
(209) · Autumn/Winter 2001-2002—photographer Jock Sturges, model Delphine.
(210) · Dress in golden embroidery from the Spring/Summer 2002 collection—photographer Federico Berardi.
(211) · Spring/Summer 2002—photographer Craig McDean, model Natalia Vodianova (*W* magazine).
OPPOSITE · Spring/Summer 2002—personal archive, photographer unknown (*Dutch* magazine).
ABOVE · Spring/Summer 2002—self-portrait by Ami Sioux.

218

220

222

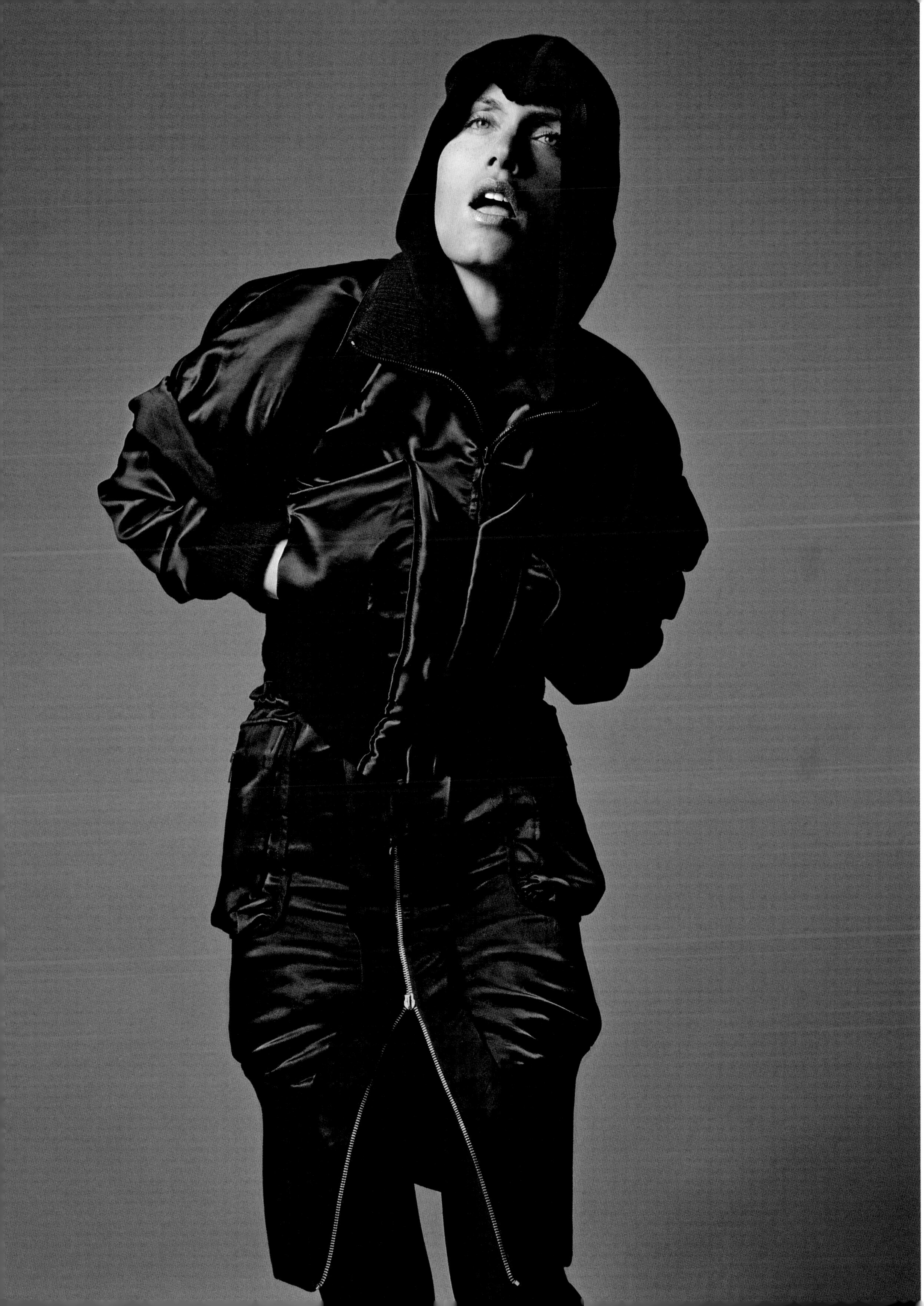

Gabrielle and Linda "with two heads" . . . research and development in the atelier for the "Trapéziste/Sport" collection, Spring/Summer 2003.

SHOT #4

E

F

G

H

228

ABOVE · Autumn/Winter 2003-2004—photographer Corinne Day (*i-D* magazine).
OPPOSITE · Dress from the Autumn/Winter 2003-2004 collection—photographer Federico Berardi.
FOLLOWING PAGES
(230) · Dress from the Autumn/Winter 2003-2004 collection—photographer Federico Berardi.
(231) · Autumn/Winter 2003-2004—photographer Vanina Sorrenti, model Rie Rasmussen.
(232-233) · Dress from the Autumn/Winter 2003-2004 collection—photographer Federico Berardi.
(234-235) · Autumn/Winter 2003-2004—photographer Vanina Sorrenti, model Rie Rasmussen.
(236) · Personal notebook, Autumn/Winter 2003-2004 collection, casting Polaroids and inspiration images.
(237) · Dress from the Autumn/Winter 2003-2004 collection—photographer Federico Berardi.
(238-239) · Autumn/Winter 2000-2001—photographer Nathaniel Goldberg, model Anouck Lepère.

230

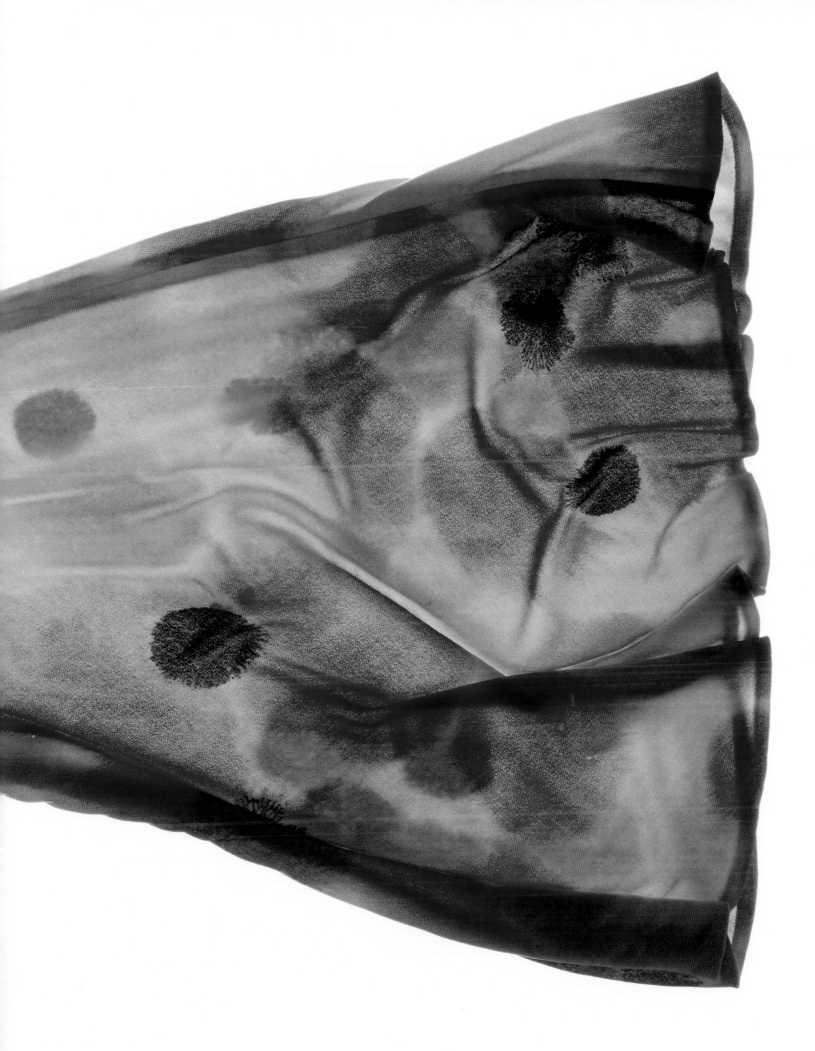

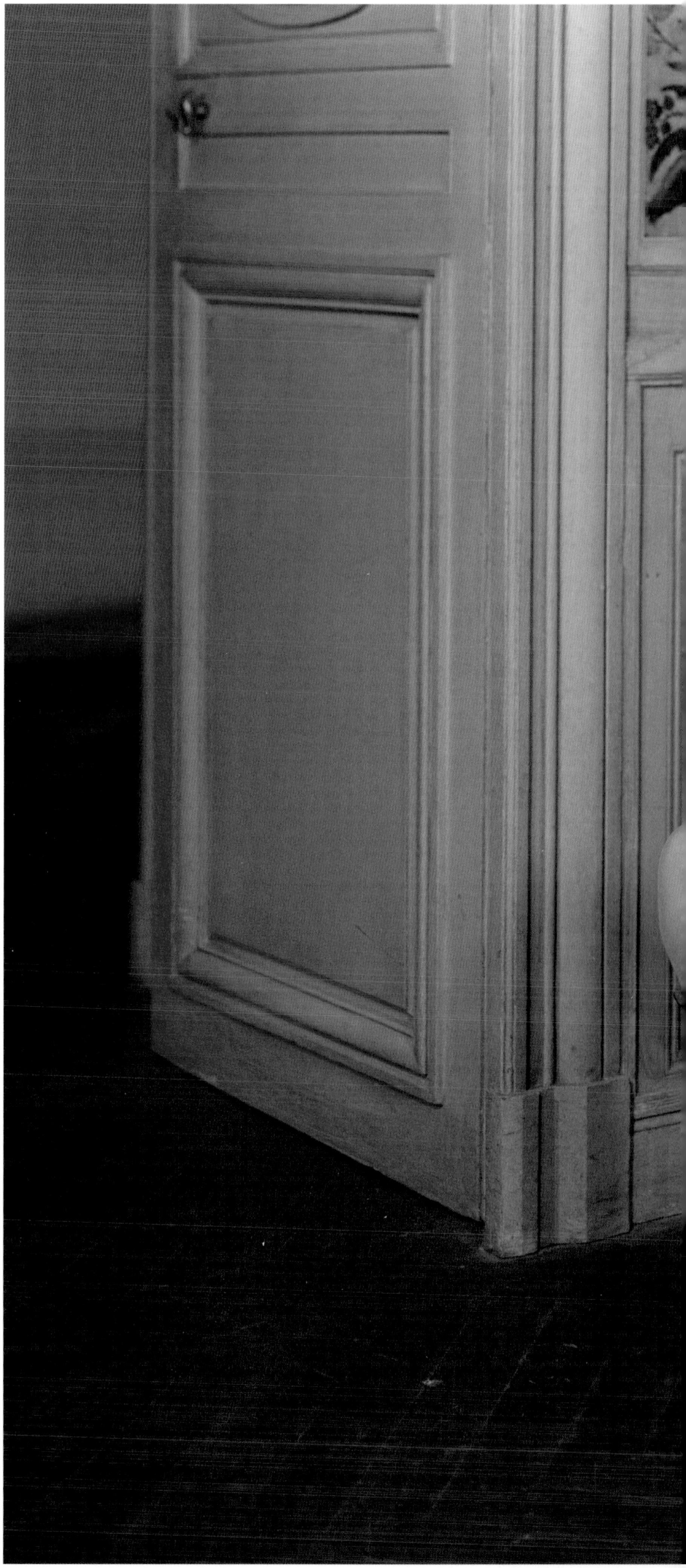

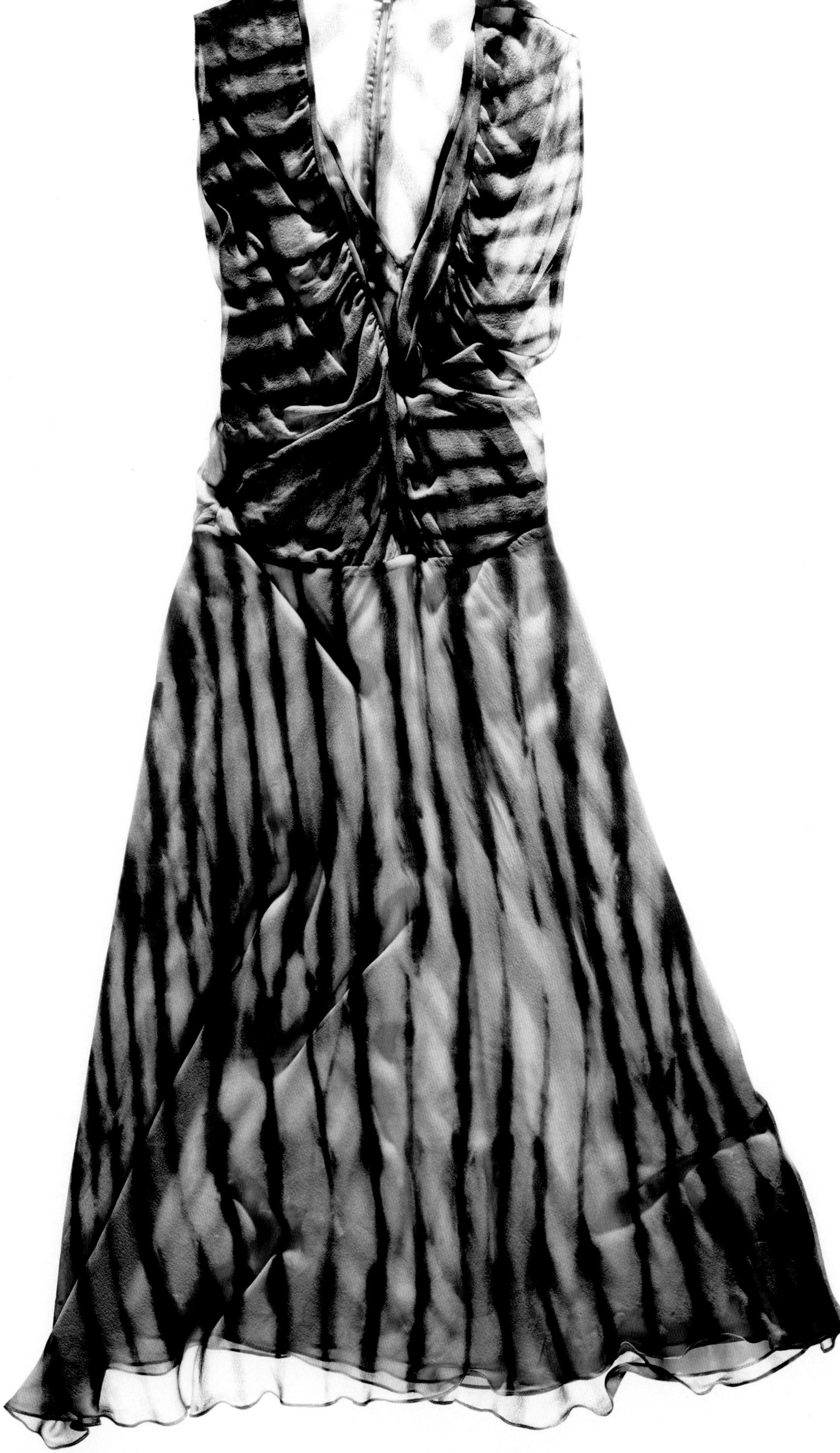

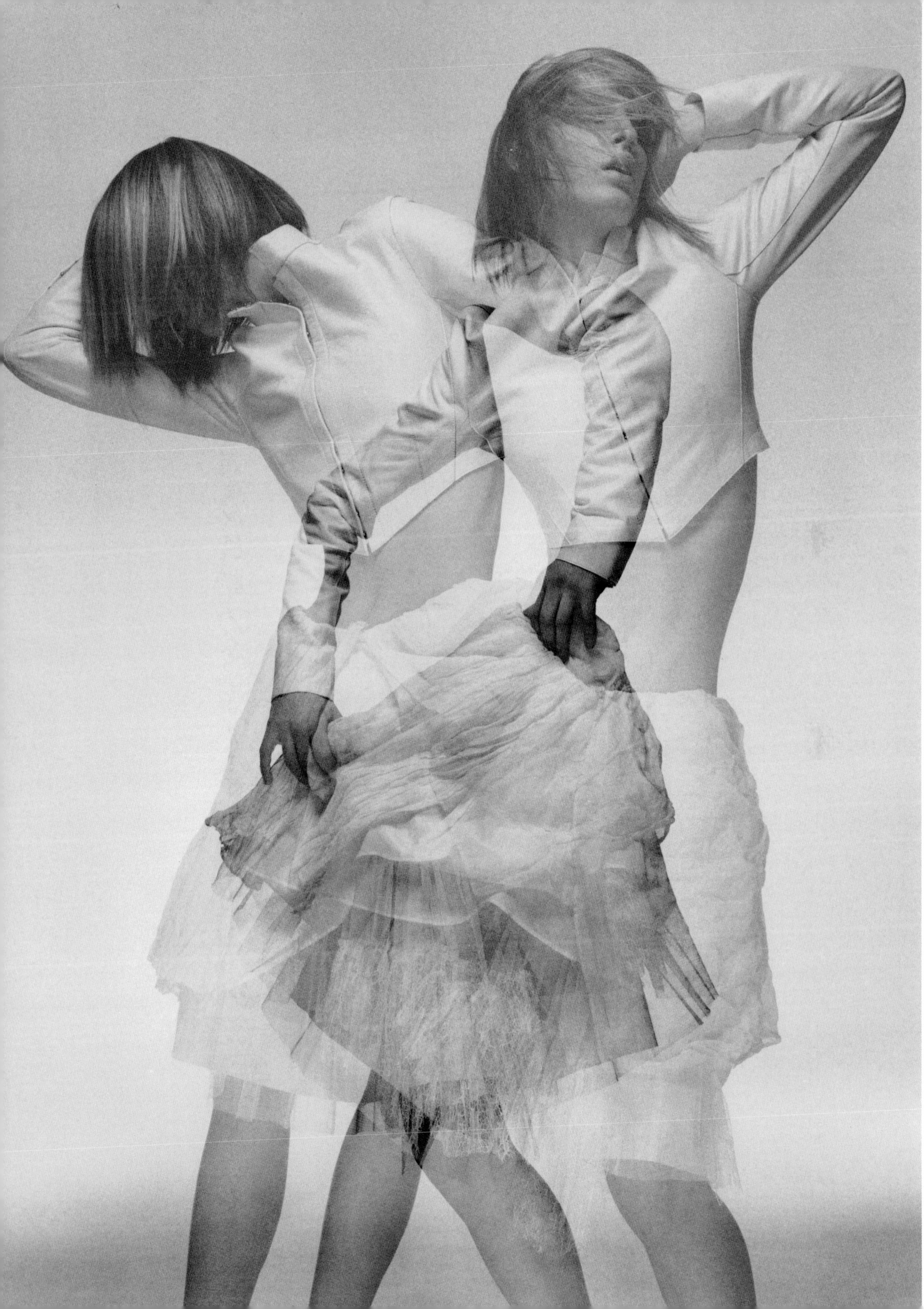

We fell in love with Lily Cole, who had just arrived from London at the last minute.

242

PREVIOUS PAGES

(240) · Personal notebook, Spring/Summer 2004 collection, Polaroids of fittings and inspiration images.

(241) · Spring/Summer 2004—photographer Sølve Sundsbø, model Natasha Vojnovic (*Numéro* France).

ABOVE AND OPPOSITE · Spring/Summer 2004—personal archives of Lily Cole photographed backstage (German *Vogue*).

FOLLOWING PAGES · Spring/Summer 2004—personal notebook with casting Polaroids of Karen Elson, Missy Rayder, Caroline, Luca, and inspiration images.

243

46

ELISE

KAREN.

51

MADELEINE

The Cockettes

Polaroid of Martine by Ezra Petronio (*Self Service* magazine).

THE RUE DU MAIL EPISODE

Fabrice Paineau

A story always has an epilogue, and Martine Sitbon's story does not end with a date, a house, or a thought, but moves on to a new address: Rue du Mail.

In 2005, Martine Sitbon lost the "Martine Sitbon" brand, which remained in the hands of her Korean partner, who developed bags and accessories. Although the body of the brand had crossed continents, its soul remained in Paris, where Martine Sitbon met Jimmy K. Chan. Together they decided to embark on a new adventure, namely Rue du Mail. There was an incredible space right in the center of Paris, near the Place des Victoires. In this new place, she invented more personal couture dreams—those of a female designer who loves her work.

Let's describe this place as a large atelier where Parisian women with good taste could ring the bell, be invited in for a conversation, and find a fitting room that was not a raft of loneliness for the senses. Modern merchandising lacks qualities and is leaning towards uniformity. Rue du Mail is a small house, a new hive of activity where, in the on-site atelier, those close to the designer transform into an un-warped creature interested in the cultural infusions of the capital. Educated by the white stones of the city, its modernity, and its never-ending movement, these women find refuge here. Her wardrobe is sensible in that it does not aim to follow the insanity of trends at all costs, but is the fruit of the designer's personality. Martine defines a girl-turned-woman enamored with craftsmanship and clothes that do not want to

248

The entrance for Rue du Mail.

ABOVE AND OPPOSITE · Photographer Sylvie Becquet, Rue du Mail (*Côté Paris*).

FOLLOWING PAGES

(250) · Martine Sitbon for Rue du Mail—Autumn/Winter 2007-2008—drawing by Cédric Rivrain.

(251) · Martine Sitbon for Rue du Mail—Autumn/Winter 2007-2008—photographer Jean-François Lepage, model Irina Lazareanu.

(253) · Martine Sitbon for Rue du Mail—Autumn/Winter 2007-2008, model Irina Lazareanu.

(254-257) · Martine Sitbon for Rue du Mail—Spring/Summer 2008—photographer Jean-François Lepage.

compete with the industrial conformity of the era. There is a desire for independence, the desire of an intellectual with no complexes who is free to create her own style. She is not dictated by the mood of the seasons that have become perennial at a time when everything is speeding up.

The gazar dresses and graphic prints give her an eclecticism that resonates widely with the complexity of this megalopolis caught between the past and the present. For a woman who lived a rock and roll youth, Rue du Mail prompts her to dedicate a specific amount of time to finding the right balance without forgetting the city that made her. As artistic director of the house, Martine continues to express her most personal choices. Her clothes have character. Just like she does.

252

ABOVE · Spring/Summer 2008—inspiration and runway photos from the second collection for Rue du Mail.
FOLLOWING PAGES
(260) · Dress from the Spring/Summer 2011 collection—photographer Federico Berardi.
(261) · Martine Sitbon for Rue du Mail—Spring/Summer 2011—photographer Javier Vallhonrat, model Suvi Koponen.

266

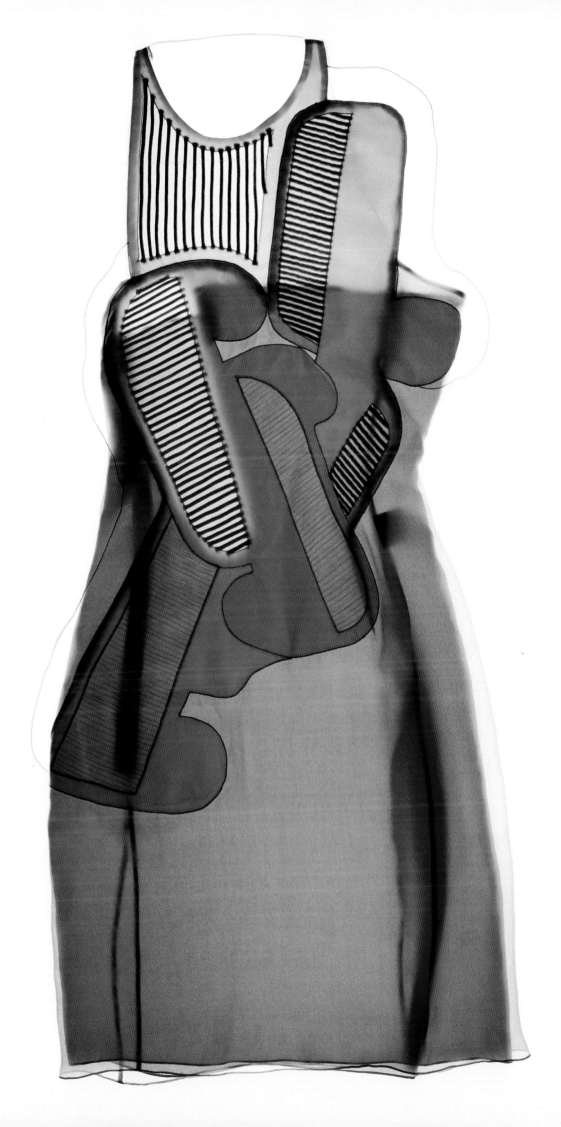

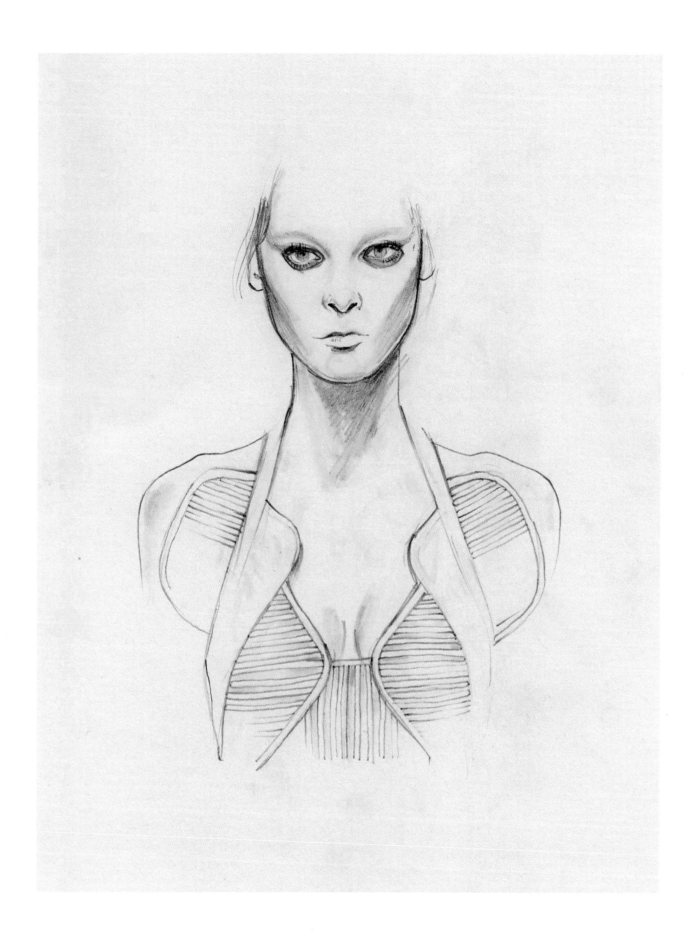

268

PREVIOUS PAGES

(262, 264-265) · Martine Sitbon for Rue du Mail—Autumn/Winter 2010-2011—self-portrait by Ami Sioux.

(263) · Martine Sitbon for Rue du Mail—Autumn/Winter 2011-2012—photographer C. G. Watkins (*Novembre* magazine).

(266) · Dress from the Spring/Summer 2011 collection.

(267) · Dress from the Spring/Summer 2009 collection—photographer Federico Berardi.

ABOVE · Martine Sitbon for Rue du Mail—Autumn/Winter 2008-2009—drawing by Cédric Rivrain.

OPPOSITE · Martine Sitbon for Rue du Mail—Autumn/Winter 2008-2009—photographer Fabien Baron (*Interview* magazine).

FOLLOWING PAGES · Martine Sitbon for Rue du Mail—Autumn/Winter 2011-2012—photographer Will Davidson, model Lindsey Wixson.

276

278

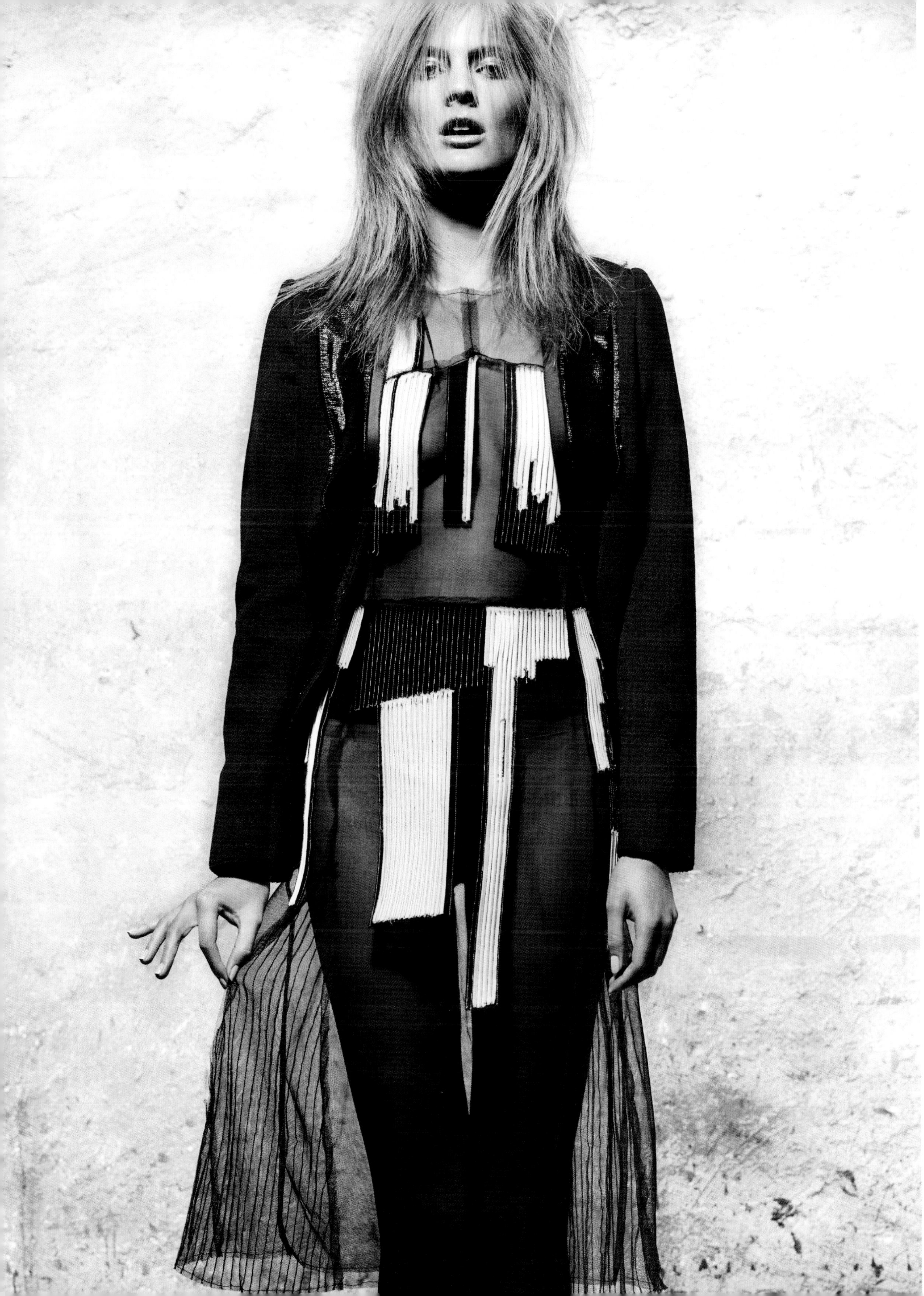

280

ABOVE · Embroidery tests on a stockman mannequin—Spring/Summer 2012 collection.
OPPOSITE · Martine Sitbon for Rue du Mail—Spring/Summer 2012—photographer Jan Welters, model Sigrid Agren (*Elle* magazine).

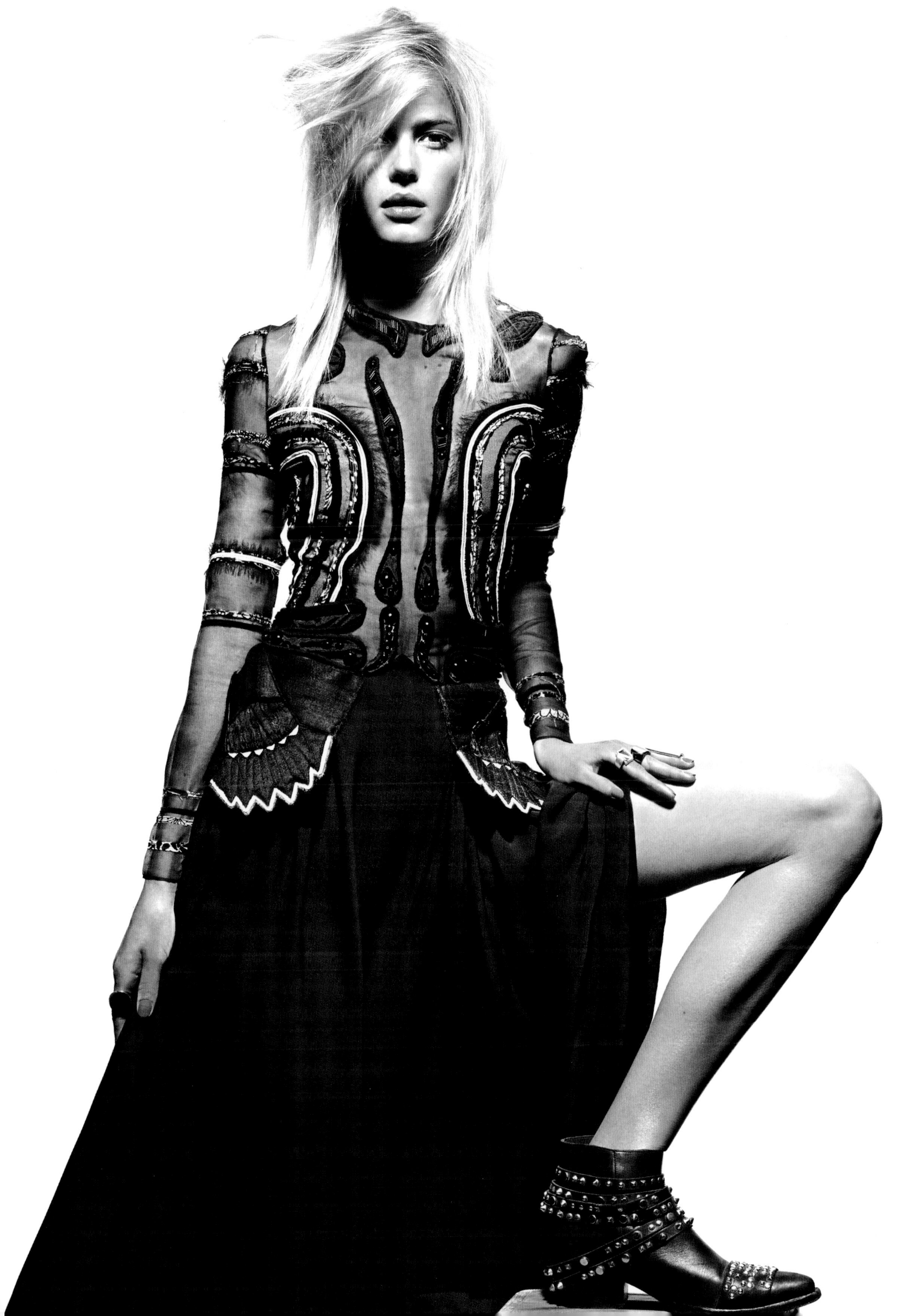

Spring/Summer 2012—embroidery development for the "Folk" collection.

286

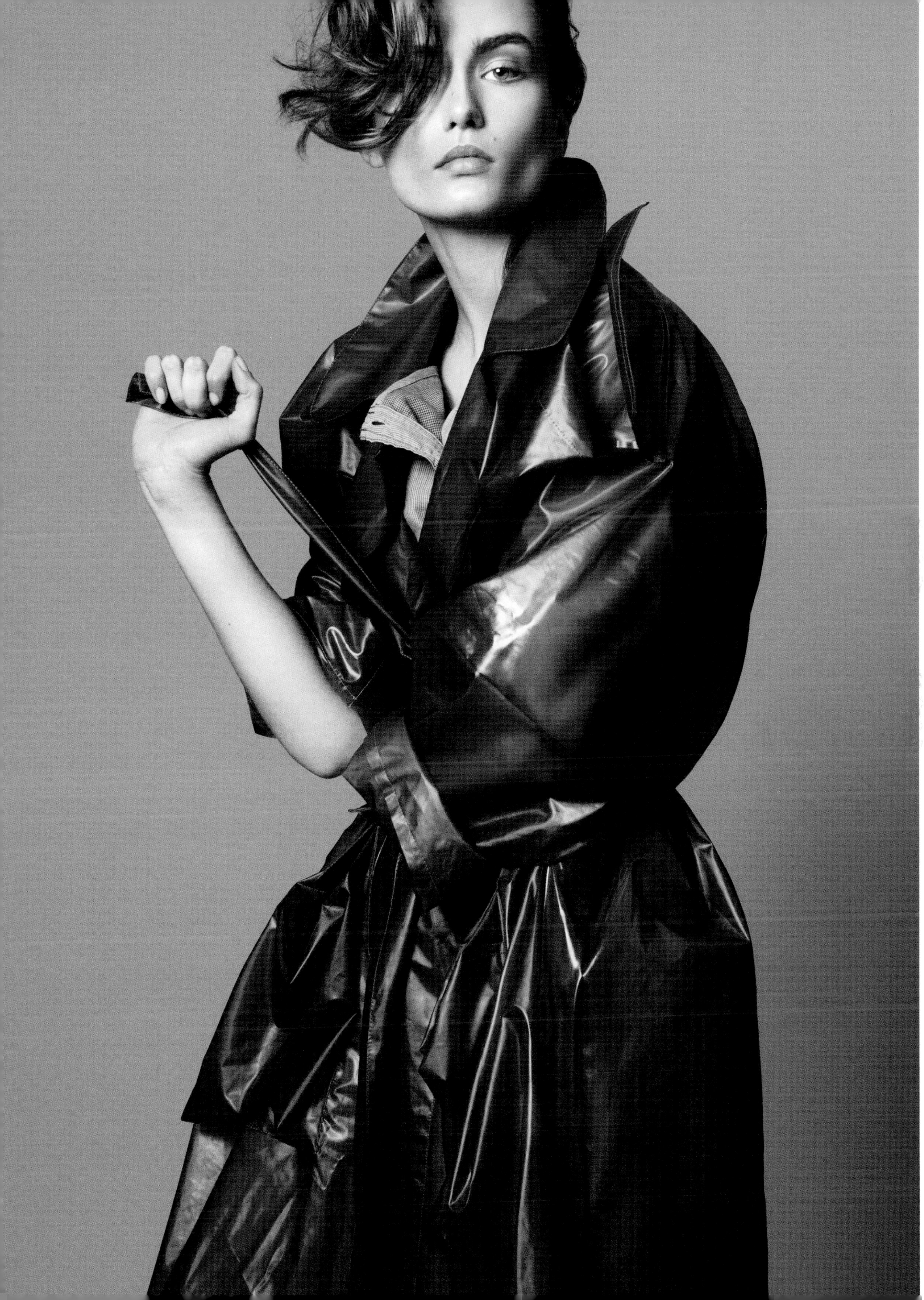

288

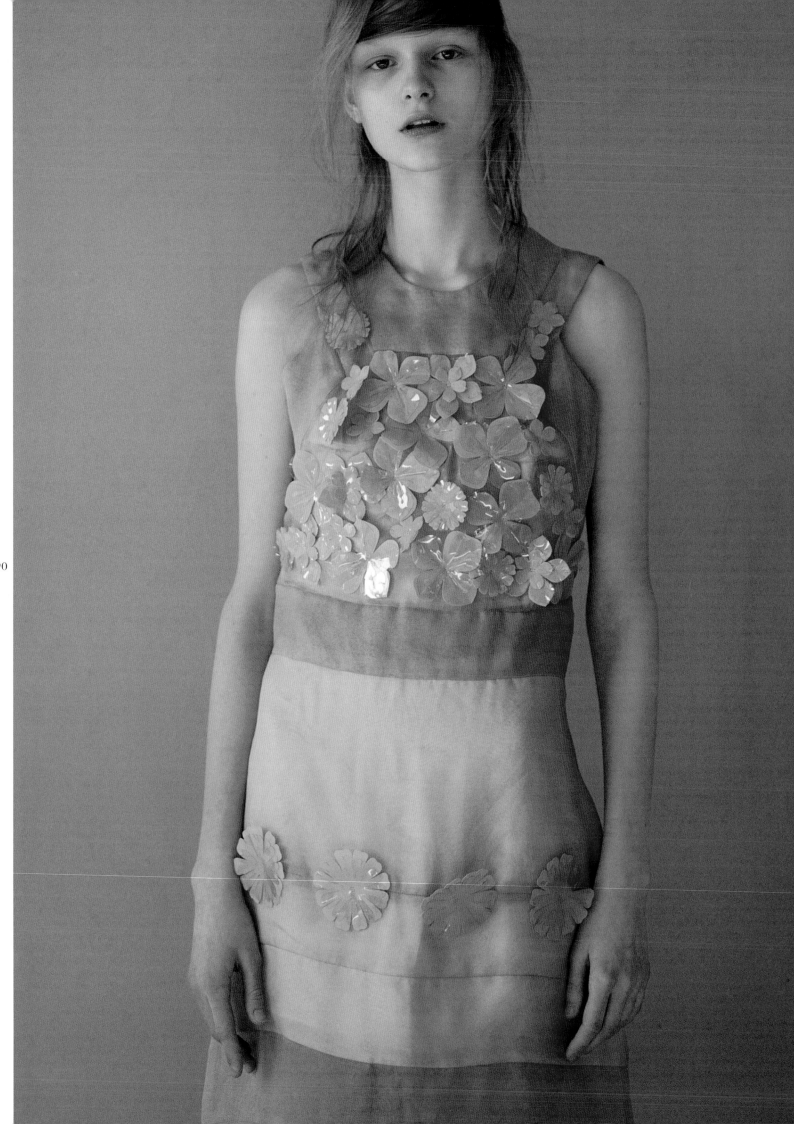

290

292

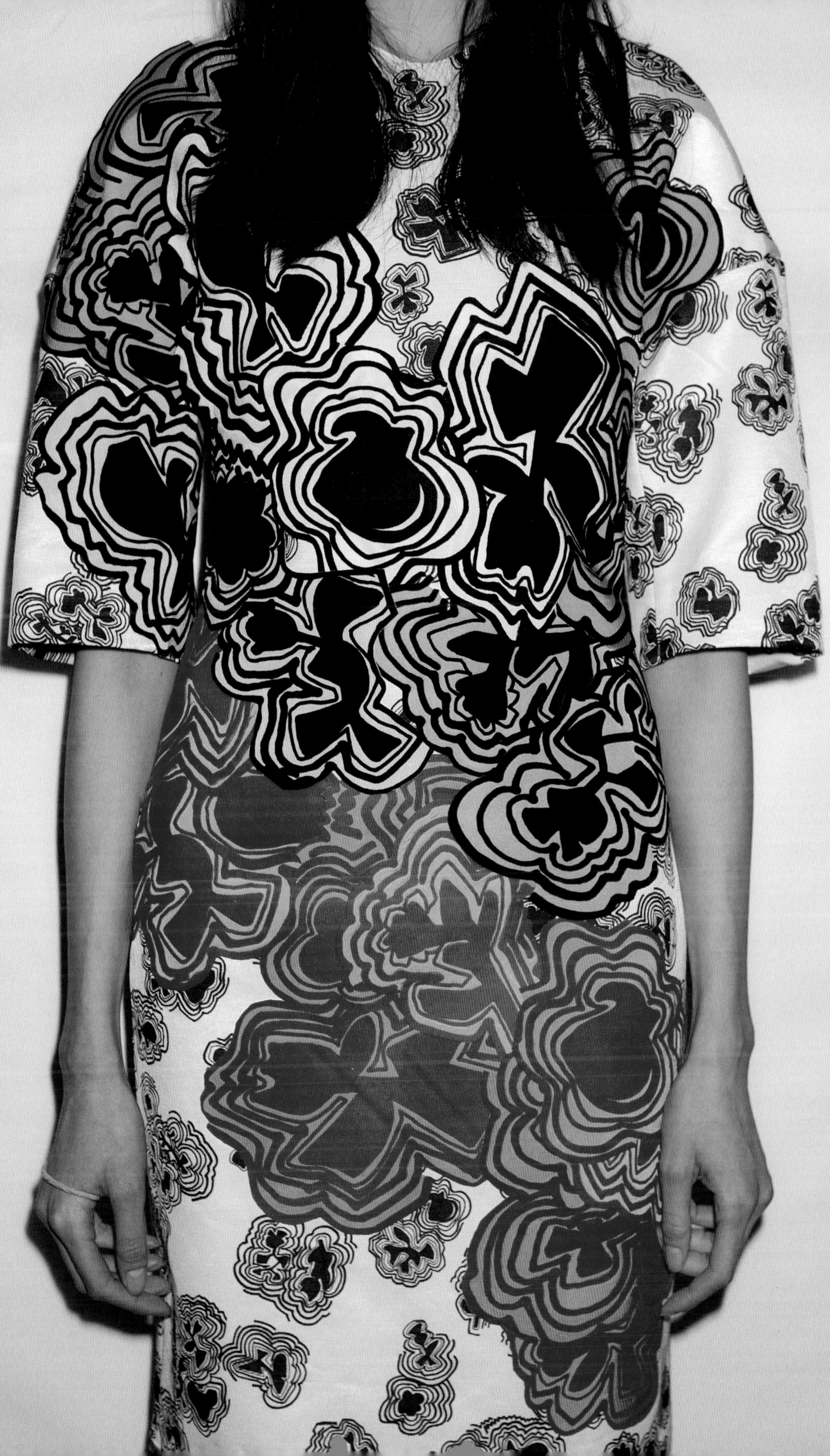

298

PREVIOUS PAGES · Martine Sitbon for Rue du Mail—Autumn/Winter 2013-2014—photographer Emma Summerton, model Catherine McNeil (Japanese *Vogue*).
ABOVE · Martine Sitbon for Rue du Mail—Autumn/Winter 2011-2012—photographers Sofia and Mauro (*Numéro* France).
OPPOSITE · Martine Sitbon for Rue du Mail—Autumn/Winter 2013-2014—photographers Sofia and Mauro.

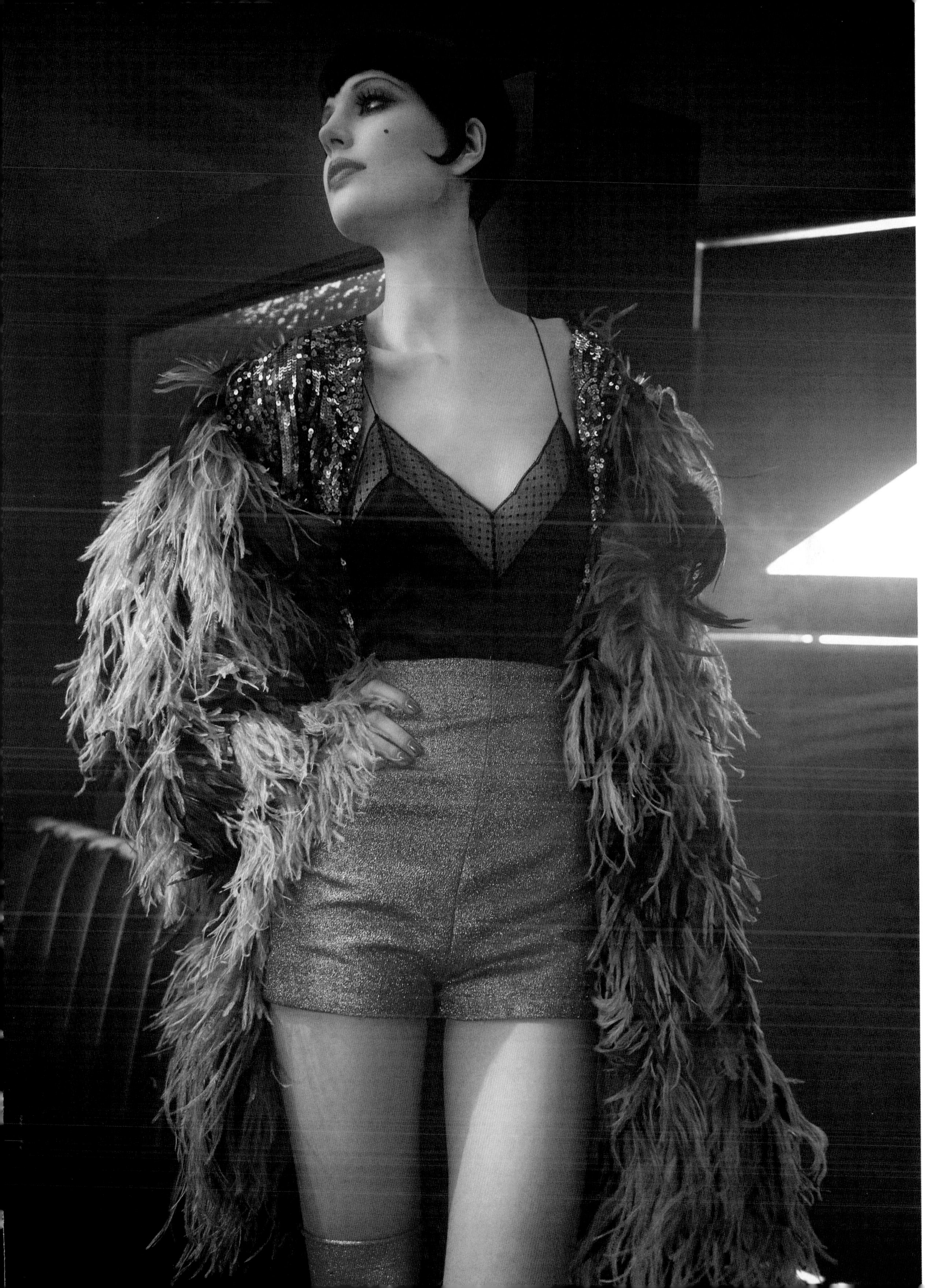

Martine Sitbon for Rue du Mail—Autumn/Winter 2013-2014—photographer Andreas Sjödin, model Doutzen Kroes.

ACKNOWLEDGMENTS

Charles Miers and Catherine Bonifassi
at Rizzoli.

Emmanuelle Alt, Camille Audibert, Michèle
Beaurenaut, Camille Bidault-Waddington, Linda
Bjork, Julie Brown, Philippe Brutus, Linda
Cantello, Marie Chaix, Lucinda Chambers,
Jimmy K. Chan, Yannick d'Is, Susanne Deeken,
Babeth Djian, Samuel François, Val Garland,
Gabrielle Greiss, Sarah Henken, Jan Kazemier,
Charlotte Knight, Titi Kwan, Brigitte Langevin,
Marc Lopez, Stéphane Marais, Joe McKenna,
Polly Mellen, Mika Mizutani, Guido Mocafico,
Michèle Montagne, Kasumiko Murakami, Masha
Orlov, Nathalie Ours, Peter Philips, Carine
Roitfeld, Catherine Rousso, Marie Rucki, Peter
Saville, Kim Sion, Eugene Souleiman, Karl
Templer, Liz Tilberis, Charlotte Tilbury,
Topolino, Julie Verhoeven, Dominique Vinant,
Melanie Ward, Patti Wilson, Aleksandra
Woroniecka, Mako Yamazaki.